A CENTURY OF MISSION AND UNITY

To
Andrew

A Century of Mission and Unity

A CENTENARY PERSPECTIVE ON THE 1910
EDINBURGH WORLD MISSIONARY CONFERENCE

Ian M. Ellis

the columba press

First edition, 2010, published by
the columba press
55A Spruce Avenue, Stillorgan Industrial Park,
Blackrock, Co Dublin

Cover by Bill Bolger
Origination by The Columba Press
Printed in Ireland by
Colour Books Ltd, Dublin

ISBN 978 1 85607 689-0

Acknowledgement
I wish to express sincere gratitude to Stephen Gregory, librarian
of Union Theological College, Belfast, for his very kind assistance
during my research for this book.

Contents

CHAPTER ONE

The Vision and Context of the Conference

'A vision of Earth! Known as a unit in this our day; every day more and more closely and organically knit by the nerves of electric cable and telegraph wire; more richly fed by the arteries and veins of railway-line and steamship ocean-way: one nation in extremest Orient thrilling at the words of some orator at the furthest sun-setting, almost as they drop from his lips; so that its inhabitants, for all the differences of tribe and race, become daily more convinced of the unity of their humanity: – one world, waiting, surely, for who shall carry to it and place in its empty hands one faith – the only thing that can ever truly and fundamentally unite it or deeply and truly satisfy it, bringing its one human race into one catholic church, through the message of the

One Body and One Spirit,
One Lord, one Faith, one Baptism,
One God and Father of all, who is over all, and through all, and in all.'

These words are to be found in the 'Introit' to W. H. T. Gairdner's account of the World Missionary Conference held in Edinburgh in 1910.[1] They sum up how Gairdner – a former Christian Union travelling secretary, missionary in Cairo and writer on mission and on Islam – saw the vision of the conference: the vision of making Christ, who fully unites, known to the entire world which was now conscious as never before of its essential unity; and, what is more, the vision was not only of one world and one faith, but also of one

1. W.H.T. Gairdner, *'Edinburgh 1910' – An account and interpretation of the World Missionary Conference*, Edinburgh and London: Oliphant, Anderson & Ferrier, 1910, p 6

church. Because the gospel itself unites people of every background, and because the communication of the gospel is seen as uniting the world, so the church itself must be a church that is truly one.

Undoubtedly, the global circumstances of the day provided an impetus for this religious awareness and set the broader context in which the missionary movement became so urgent and organised. The church does not live for itself and the course of church events is usually influenced – at some times more so than at others – by developments in the wider world. Time and again this reality has been made clear in the history of the church. Naturally, at times there are conflicts between how the world sees issues and how the churches wish to respond, but the two realms – the sacred and the secular – are not wholly divorced from each other, are not somehow sealed off from each other so that what happens in the secular world is of no relevance to church life. On the contrary, secular events repeatedly can be seen to have been the catalyst for major changes in church life. That is certainly true, for example, in the modern European context, where a Europe that has been coming together in remarkable ways since the Second World War has doubtlessly led to much closer relationships between the churches in Europe (including Ireland and Britain). The influence of secular circumstances on church life is certainly to be seen in the missionary movement as the nineteenth century gave way to a vastly different twentieth century.

The progress of industrialisation in the nineteenth century, first in Britain and then in western Europe and the United States of America, had led to an immense economic – and military – superiority of those nations over the unindustrialised world. The expansion of western imperialism across the globe was a consequence of this imbalance. This was also a time of considerable population growth in Europe and of increasing prosperity and, indeed, of the beginnings of effective social welfare provision; the nineteenth century also saw, in Britain, the real beginnings of a women's movement, although emancipation was not to advance until the following century. The industrialisation of the nineteenth century saw the increasing exploitation of trade routes, which gathered pace with the development of steamships, railways, the internal combustion engine and electricity. The economist, Angus Maddison, has indicated that by the 1920s the British Empire embraced one-quarter of the world's population.[2]

To read Gairdner's account of Edinburgh 1910 is to realise that there truly was a vision of one world, won for Christ; the expansion of western political influence clearly engendered a confidence that this was also a time of real spiritual opportunity. While Robert Knox's book, *The Races of Man*, published in 1850, had signalled a rise in race thinking which expounded race as the basis of civilisation, and in a sense contradicted the 'one world' view, the subsequent Christian missionary attitude was typically that of the 'trusteeship' outlook. This, while accepting the concept of racial differentiation, for example saw the British Empire as existing not to promote jingoism or triumphalism but to confer benefits on its peoples to assist their development.[3]

A. C. Ross writes of the issue of racism in relation to mission: 'Until the 1850s, [the] belief in the oneness of humanity was widespread; it was a powerful influence on many, though not all, evangelical Protestants on both sides of the Atlantic. An unambiguous statement of this belief was the constitution that the American Antislavery Society adopted at its inaugural meeting in 1833. This document called not only for the immediate freeing of the slaves but also for them to receive full civil rights as US citizens.'[4] He points out that the belief in the essential equality of all human beings, irrespective of race, is clearly proclaimed in the writings of John Philip, the resident director of the London Missionary Society in southern Africa from 1819-1851, who wrote in a letter to the American Board of Commissioners for Foreign Missions: 'So far as my observation extends, it appears to me that

2. A. Maddison, *The World Economy: A millennial perspective*, OECD, 2001, pp 98, 242

3. Cf A. C. Ross, *Christian Missions and the Mid-Nineteenth Century Change in Attitudes to Race: The African Experience*, in. ed A. Porter, *The Imperial Horizons of British Protestant Missions, 1880-1914*, Grand Rapids and Cambridge: Eerdmans, 2003 ('Studies in the History of Christian Missions' series), p 90, and D. W. Bebbington, *Atonement, Sin and Empire, 1880-1914*, ibid., p 30

4. A. C. Ross, op. cit., p 87

the natural capacity of the African is nothing inferior to that of the European. At our schools, the children of Hottentots, of Bushmen, of Caffres and of the Bechuanas, are in no respect behind the capacity of those of European parents: and the people at our missionary stations are in many instances superior in intelligence to those who look down upon them.'[5]

However, Knox's race thinking typified the view of humanity that was swiftly rising in the second half of the nineteenth century and held sway until the 1930s. In that period it was understood as 'scientific', but today is described as 'pseudoscientific'. It was a terrible mistake at the heart of the Western intelligentsia. Ross stresses that the trusteeship approach to the subject, which was typical in the missionary movement, far from endorsing any ill treatment of 'inferior' races, nonetheless emphasised the responsibilities of the 'superior' towards the 'inferior'.[6]

The growth of such race perspectives in the nineteenth century, which essentially contradicted Christianity's tenet of human equality, in fact led both to an undermining of the missionary enterprise and to a weakening of the Empire. So, Andrew Porter writes: 'At the beginning of the nineteenth century ... (I)t was generally held that there existed a single, divinely created, human race ... The essential conditions under-pinned the expectations of administrators and humanitarians as well as evangelicals that liberty, prosperity, civilisation and Christianity would advance together. In most quarters, this universalist outlook was gradually undermined during the nineteenth century. It was eroded by the unexpected slowness in the transformation of the extra-European world and the consequential widening of the technological gulf and the disparity in wealth between the British and indigenous peoples. Interpreted as evidence of resistance to British ways despite the benefits of long periods of British contact or rule, events such as the Indian Mutiny, West Indian decline, the Jamaican rebellion and China's Boxer Rising, led people to question the rationality or basic capacity of non-Europeans.'

---

5. In ibid., p 86
6. In ibid., p 92; Ross refers to Kipling's poem, *The White Man's Burden* (1899), as illustrating the trusteeship attitude.

However, while missions were not immune from the trend in race thinking, Porter points out that the missionary outlook in the late nineteenth century remained universalist in nature, not least because of the biblical principles of the universal dimensions of grace, redemption and atonement.[7]

Brian Stanley, in his very recent major study of Edinburgh 1910, nonetheless writes that concepts of racial distinctiveness and variation were integral to the language of the Edinburgh reports, and as an example of this writes that the Commission I report 'observed the "enormous influence" currently wielded by the white man among the "primitive races" …'[8] Indeed, addressing the conference, the Indian V. S. Azariah raised the issue of race relationships as what he described as 'one of the most serious problems confronting the church today'. Stanley notes of Azariah's address: 'It went on to complain of "a certain aloofness, a lack of mutual understanding and openness, a great lack of frank intercourse and friendliness" between European missionaries and national Christians, citing examples of experienced Indian national missionaries who had never once been invited to share a meal with any of their European brethren, and conversely of European missionaries who had never dreamt of visiting the homes of their Indian missionary colleagues. He pointed out that "Friendship is more than condescending love" and urged that, on the basis of his own experience, friendship between two very different races was possible.'[9] A main point that Azariah wanted to make was that in crossing racial boundaries the gospel of Christ could be better promoted.

Stanley also notes that the international committee that prepared for Edinburgh 1910 had suggested that missionary societies should be asked to include in their delegations, as the committee put it, 'if practicable, one or two natives from mission

---

7. A. Porter, *Religion versus empire? British Protestant missionaries and overseas expansion, 1700-1914*, Manchester University Press, 2005, pp 283-5
8. B. Stanley, *The World Missionary Conference, Edinburgh 1910*, Grand Rapids and Cambridge: Eerdmans, 2009, p 307
9. Ibid., p 102

lands', but he goes on to point out that most missions in fact failed to do so.[10]

If the church does not have a vision of a world won for Christ, its mission is hampered by self-doubt. Yet, in today's world of expanding interfaith dialogue and real mutual respect among the religions, the religious view of Gairdner and others of his day – one world united in the one Christian faith – may seem lacking in realism. Nonetheless, the report which formed the basis for Edinburgh 1910's consideration of 'The Missionary Message in Relation to the Non-Christian religions' concluded: 'The spectacle of the advance of the Christian Church along many lines of action to the conquest of the five great religions of the modern world is one of singular interest and grandeur.'[11]

What are we, today, to make of such a vision? Surely, while the church wants every person to come to know Christ, the picture of striving, by God's grace, for one world united in Christ is looking somewhat different from the perspective of one hundred years ago; that is, of course, hardly surprising. The church certainly no longer thinks in terms of the 'conquest' of other faiths – the church supremely militant – but of Christ drawing all people into union with himself and of this being aided by the church's life of loving witness. So, for example, the current mission statement of the Anglican Communion's Network for Inter-Faith Concerns, *inter alia*, encourages 'Progress towards genuinely open and loving relationships between Christians and people of other faiths' and 'Sensitive witness and evangelism where appropriate'.[12]

However, Edinburgh 1910, in considering non-Christian religion, in fact displayed an evangelistic approach that was rooted in a very considered overview of the world's religious state and a remarkably generous appreciation of the insights of other religions. After Edinburgh 1910, the nature of the approach to non-Christian religions, of course, was to become an increasingly controversial issue, and clearly remains controversial today.

The World Missionary Conference held in Edinburgh 1910 not

---

10. Ibid., p 102
11. Ibid., p 135
12. http://nifcon.anglicancommunion.org/index.cfm

only gave its own very significant impetus to a growing missionary movement, but also gave birth to the modern ecumenical movement, and this will be considered further in later chapters. The 1910 conference in fact styled itself 'ecumenical', but only in the sense of being truly representative of the whole inhabited world (the *oikumene*) and not in the common, modern sense of 'ecumenical'. Edinburgh 1910 was first and foremost a missionary conference; mission was its purpose and focus. However, it did not simply appear from nowhere, but followed earlier international missionary conferences, not least London (1888) and New York (1900). There had thus been a developing co-operation among Protestant missionary societies and Edinburgh 1910 stands in that line, although with its own distinctive approach.

The missionary movement had been developing in the nineteenth century; its thrust was in voluntary groups and organisations on both sides of the Atlantic. A major driving element was the Evangelical Awakening. Referring to the different origins of the Evangelical Awakening in different countries, Ruth Rouse has written: 'In Germany, the Evangelical Revival can be traced to the Pietist movement in the eighteenth century and its successors in the nineteenth. In Britain its impulse came largely, though not wholly, from the evangelistic efforts of the Wesleys and Whitfield and the rise of Methodism. In America it arose from the Great Awakening of the eighteenth century and the nineteenth century response of the churches to the spiritual needs of the frontier. But whatever its origins, its spirit and its underlying motives were always the same. Its passion was evangelism – evangelism at home and to the ends of the earth.'[13]

The Evangelical Awakening was a movement that brought new life and vigour to the church. In a world that was opening up to travel and communication, the possibilities for the proclamation of the gospel seemed to be endless and young Christians, fired with both idealism and faith, were moved to serve in the great endeavour. There was indeed a passion for evangelical outreach, and a real sense of its urgency.

13. Ed R. Rouse and S. Neill, *A History of the Ecumenical Movement: 1517-1948,* London: SPCK, 1948, p 309

Missionary organisations had taken shape by the early nineteenth century and it was clear that co-operation would be vital;
Rouse has noted that there was even a degree of sharing, however
informal, between Protestant and Roman Catholic missionaries.[14] However, it is true, if somewhat strange, that the missionary
emphasis was not really marked in the churches of the
Reformation until the 1790s and the nineteenth century, when the
societies emerged and were organised with considerable enthusiasm: in Britain, the first being the Baptist Missionary Society in
1792, the interdenominational London Missionary Society in
1795 and the Church Missionary Society in 1799.[15] The immediate
concerns of the churches of the Reformation were not global in
nature; they were more nationally focused institutions. This
changed, however, as the world opened up and as a result of the
Evangelical Awakening.

The involvement of students in the Student Volunteer
Missionary Union was crucial to the advance of the missionary
movement. Tissington Tatlow, in his monumental history of the
Student Christian Movement, points out that the Student
Volunteer Movement was already well established in America by
the end of the nineteenth century. Its spread to Britain and Ireland
was to a great extent helped by the efforts of the American, Robert
Wilder, whose father was both founder and editor of *The
Missionary Review of the World*, a monthly publication with a truly
comprehensive approach.[16]

The American dimension and indeed impulse to the developing missionary movement is crucial, and to understand it one
needs to consider a certain American perspective in the later nineteenth and early twentieth centuries. The United States at this
time was already the wealthiest country in the world, the land of
opportunity and a place for initiative. The historian, Paul
Johnson, in his very substantial *History of the American People*,

---

14. Ibid., p 313
15. cf J. Wolff, *God and Greater Britain: Religion and National Life in Britain
and Ireland, 1843-1945*, London & New York: Routledge, 1994, p 215
16. cf T. Tatlow, *The Story of the Student Christian Movement*, London:
SCM, 1933, p 22

sums up the characteristics of America with which we are familiar today, and which he points out were beginning to take shape already by the end of the Civil War (1861-65): 'huge and teeming, endlessly varied, multicoloured and multiracial, immensely materialistic and overwhelmingly idealistic, ceaselessly innovative, thrusting, grabbing, buttonholing, noisy, questioning, anxious to do the right thing, to do good, to get rich, to make everybody happy'.[17] Welcome to America. Perhaps this is fair, or unfair, but certainly the truth is recognisable amongst the adjectives that here is a nation that is so vibrant that it surely must influence the world decisively.

Johnson explores the unique American frontier experience. The frontier, defined as 'land occupied by two or more but less than six persons, on average, per square mile',[18] advanced to the west from the 1860s to the 1880s, coming to an end by 1890. It had been a time of free-for-all, not least in religion. So, mission was at the heart of the American experience as America developed into the nation that it was at the turn of the century. The United States was a place where people were self-made, where absolute fortunes were achievable and where talent could flourish. It was a nation of industry that led to the creation of new cities with their great skyscrapers, symbols of determination to reach for the sky in every sense. And the United States was a nation of faith.

American faith reached out with the same driving commitment that characterised the nation's own self-creation. Johnson writes of the late nineteenth century: 'By this stage America was the leading missionary force, in terms of the resources it deployed, especially in Asia and the Pacific, and it was thought that the white races in general, and the Anglo-Saxons in particular, would succeed in bringing to reality Christ's vision of nearly two millennia before – a universal faith. The nineteenth century had been a period of such astonishing, and on the whole benign, progress that even this great dream now seemed possible. In the 1880s the young American Methodist John Raleigh Mott had

---

17. P. Johnson, *A History of the American People*, London: Weidenfeld & Nicholson, 1997, p 425
18. Ibid., p 435

coined the phrase "The evangelising of the world in one generation". That was a task for American leadership.'[19] Mott was, in
fact, to chair Edinburgh 1910.

Andrew Porter has pointed to the Young Men's Christian
Association, founded in 1844, as a common root for the Student
Volunteer Movement in America and the British Student
Volunteer Missionary Union, and has commented: 'The significance of the SVM for British – not to mention worldwide – missionary enterprise was enormous. More than anything else in the
1890s it was the chief source of fresh ideas and enthusiasm for the
traditional overseas societies. It generated recruits, funds and inspiration sufficient to survive even the great hiatus and missionary reconstruction imposed by the war of 1914-18.'[20]

In 1896, the Student Volunteer Missionary Union held its first
international students' conference in Liverpool. Tatlow records
that for over two years, leaders of the Union were concerned that
the churches as institutions had not been responding at all adequately to the growing missionary interest in the colleges. So, one
of the main purposes of the Liverpool conference was, Tatlow
writes, to make 'a demonstration of the strength of the Movement
as a challenge to the Church'.[21] Moreover, at this conference and
under the influence of the American movement, the 'Watchword',
which clearly goes straight back to J. R. Mott, was adopted: 'The
Evangelisation of the world in this generation'. This, Tatlow observes, had given 'inspiration and edge' to the Volunteer
Movement in America.

However, when the SVMU expounded the Watchword in *The
Student Volunteer*, it was emphasised that 'evangelisation' was
not understood as 'Christianisation': 'The aim is to bring Christ
within the reach of every individual that he may have an opportunity of intelligently accepting him as a personal Saviour.'[22] The
key issue was not whether the objective was inherently achievable but whether it was in fact organisationally possible, a matter

19. Ibid., p 508
20. A. Porter, op. cit., pp 301 & 305
21. Tatlow, op. cit., p 69
22. Ibid., p 105

that actually gave rise to considerable calculations as to the number of missionaries needed for the task. Writing in *The Student Volunteer* in 1897, G. T. Manley of Cambridge University declared that it was indeed possible to reach every human being within the current generation, estimating that 6,000 missionaries would be needed to reach the 200 million people in Africa. He expounded his estimate that 'thirty-three thousand Western Christians, if volunteering within the next five years, would be a minimum sufficient to lead the forces of the Native Churches in a great Movement for the Evangelisation of the World in this generation'.[23] In the final in his series of four articles, Manley dismissed any suggestion that the Watchword was presumptuous or not possible. Also in 1897, Rutter Williamson (who had a particular interest in medical missions) made the issue as clear as it could be: 'As a Union we believe that the Watchword expresses, not merely an ideal, but states a present duty of the church, which, if realised as such, is easily possible of accomplishment ... it is not a mere quickening of interest in missions we seek. It is a definite, sustained and comprehensive appropriation of the opportunities presented before us today for evangelising the whole world *in this our generation.*'[24] [Italics original]

Certainly from the perspective of the British and Irish Student Missionary Volunteer Movement, the goal was the communication of the gospel, but this was not born of a vision of religious domination. The opportunity to tell the whole world the good news of Christ was there and, because the opportunity was there, it simply had to be taken up. Anything less was seen as sheer faithlessness. What was seen as opportunity instantly became an undoubted duty. For that reason, the student movement set out to shake the church out of any complacency and sought to awaken all to the task that was necessary if Christian people were to be true to their faith and calling. A time of opportunity demanded the response of faith expressed in personal sacrifice and commitment to play one's part in the great missionary endeavour. There was a supremely personal appeal and challenge in this clarion

---

23. As in Ibid., p 107

24. *The Student Volunteer*, Summer 1897, p 80. As in ibid., p 108

call: the world awaited the hearing of the good news, and the good news could only be proclaimed if there were individuals who would give of themselves and go wherever they were called. St Paul's words could have been the motto: 'How then shall they call on him in whom they have not believed? and how shall they believe in him whom they have not heard? and how shall they hear without a preacher?' (Rom 10:14)

W. H. T. Gairdner was invited by the committee of the 1910 Edinburgh World Missionary Conference to 'write up' the experience from his own perspectives. He makes it clear that, while the conference stood in a succession of previous international general conferences (in 1854, 1860, 1878, 1888 and 1900), the aim of Edinburgh was not to be a showcase of mission. There was no desire to use the occasion to stir up a general interest in mission, not least because there was no doubt that such a gathering could only have a relatively limited reach as a showcase. Rather, it was decided by the preparatory committee that the purpose of Edinburgh 1910 should be strategic. There was a sense, after some one hundred years of activity by the missionary organisations, that their successes in Africa and Asia opened up real vistas of opportunity. Advances had been achieved, but they served to emphasise how much more there was to be done – and there was, as we have seen, a real confidence at the end of the nineteenth and beginning of the twentieth centuries that the ways that seemed to lie open were fertile ground for the seed of the gospel, and that the seed could be brought everywhere, if only there were enough volunteers. The gathering at Edinburgh in 1910 was therefore not simply to tell what was going on in the mission field but was to plan, and to plan most methodically in the spirit of the Watchword, for the evangelisation of the world – even if the meaning of that term might have had somewhat different nuances in different quarters.[25] In the preparation for Edinburgh 1910 there was a very involved and somewhat protracted debate amongst the organisers

---

25. In this connection it may be noted that the Archbishop of Canterbury, Edward White Benson, referred to the 'Christianisation of God's earth' in his last sermon, preached in St Patrick's Church of Ireland Cathedral, Armagh (27 September, 1896). cf Tatlow, op. cit., p 133

on both sides of the Atlantic as to whether missions to essentially Roman Catholic or Orthodox countries should be included within the overall purview of the conference. Very largely due to Anglican influence, and the desire of non-Anglicans to secure Anglican participation at Edinburgh 1910, it was decided, as Stanley writes, that 'Protestant proselytism of Roman Catholics, and, rather less clearly of Orthodox and Oriental Christians' should be no valid part of Christian mission. However, Stanley also points out that this implied 'the division of humanity into two along lines that were not strictly confessional, but primarily geographical'.[26]

Gairdner sees what we today would term a decisive geopolitical change as having taken place with the Battle of Mukden shortly before the end of the Russo-Japanese war (1904-05). The change signalled by Mukden lay in the fact that this was the first defeat of a European power by an Asian power in modern times. Gairdner interprets the event thus: 'Up to that time [the ushering in of the twentieth century], from the earliest days of European commerce with the Orient ... the tides of empire and domination, of political and commercial supremacy, had rolled from the West to East ... And then Port Arthur fell, the Battle of Moukden [sic] was fought, the Trafalgar of the Korean Straights was decided; and the entire aspect of things was changed ... The tide of western dominance and domination, which had seemed more like an unchangeable phenomenon of nature than a resultant of human actions and states, was checked, rolled suddenly back.'

This geopolitical change Gairdner interprets as a moment of awakening of consciousness of the oneness of the world, but with a sense of fear of all the potential for a major clash of civilisations, Asian and European/American, in somehow seeking to settle that global unity. One world together, yes, but one world at peace? An alternative was that the whole world should be civilised and made truly peaceable in the faith of Christ.[27]

The fear of war was, surely, a real part of the consciousness of the time. Europe in the eighteenth century had avoided major

26. Op. cit .p 72
27. Gairdner, op. cit., pp 9ff

conflicts, but the century had seen the rise of nationalism across the continent, perhaps due not least, and somewhat paradoxically, to wider suffrage which gave people an increased stake in, and therefore pride in, their own countries. In this nationalism lay a great danger to the peace, precisely because it meant that national interests began to compete in earnest and, when taken to its extremes, small disputes could become more serious than they really were. This rise of nationalism weakened the eastern European Austro-Hungarian, Russian and Ottoman empires as constituent states sought independence; indeed, it was in the highly volatile Balkans that the assassination of the heir to the Austro-Hungarian throne, the Archduke Francis Ferdinand, led to the unimaginable conflict that was the First World War.[28]

Those who had planned and gathered for Edinburgh 1910 must have had some awareness of danger looming; the nations themselves had recognised the perils of the time and had formed alliances – the military Triple Alliance between Germany, Austro-Hungary and Italy, and the more informal *Entente Cordiale* between Britain and France, Russia joining in 1907 to bring about the *Triple Entente*.

Allied to this was the fact that the increasing wealth of the western nations had led to a growing armaments industry, with the production of new warships and weapons of war and the establishment of very considerable standing armies. Towards the end of the nineteenth century, Germany's army was the most formidable anywhere in the world and, not wishing to allow too great an imbalance of power, other European nations started to build up their military capacity, although Britain relied most on its navy. However, Germany then began to expand its navy in order to become a sea power to rival Britain. The British launched the mightily armed *Dreadnought* in 1906 – it was the heaviest armed battleship of its time – but Germany responded by building battleships of similar capacity. Advances in industrial technology aided the new arms race, but there were those who held that greater capacity would mean shorter conflicts. How wrong they were.

---

28. In Sarajevo, 28th June, 1914

From the standpoint of 1910, it was scarcely credible that this would be the future – mass warfare. Was this really the destiny of humanity in the new twentieth century?

There was a different way; the world could choose the path of peace and Christian civilisation. For this to be realised, the missionary task had to be organised – and the organisation of the endeavour was urgent.

The Edinburgh 1910 preparatory committee, to which reference has been made above, first met in 1908. It established eight themes for the conference: (1) Carrying the gospel to all the non-Christian world; (2) The church in the mission field; (3) Education in relation to the Christianisation of national life; (4) The missionary message in relation to non-Christian religions; (5) The preparation of missionaries; (6) The home base of missions; (7) Relation of missions to governments; and (8) Co-operation and the promotion of unity. Eight commissions were formed under these headings and the commissions sent questionnaires to literally hundreds of missionaries in the mission field, to be returned for analysis by the commissions which then produced reports to be circulated in advance of the conference. It was an amazing process, given the relative slowness of mail communication around the world by today's standards. Gairdner atmospherically writes of the delegates' eventual journeying to Edinburgh: 'And so in railway-train, on P and O Atlantic liner, the spectacle of the long folio printed documents might have been seen, in the hands of a thousand delegates, coming from East, West, North and South, as they tried to accomplish the feat of mastering eight volumes of closest thinking ...'[29]

In this way, opportunity was seen and seized for missionary advance across the world. A strategic, business conference was called to plan the response to that opportunity. And the delegates came, prepared by the thorough work of the commissions. There simply had to be a sense of truly eager anticipation and, indeed, excitement, as everyone gathered in the Scottish capital.

---

29. Gairdner, op. cit., p 26. There were in fact 1,200 delegates at the conference.

A key and towering missionary and, ultimately, ecumenical figure at Edinburgh 1910 was John R. Mott (1865-1955), to whom reference has already been made above, who chaired the conference and had chaired the preparatory process.[30]

Mott, an American Methodist, had been involved with the international committee for the YMCA and had been chairman of the Student Volunteer Movement. As a student himself, in 1886 he had dedicated his life to making Christ known. In 1895 he became general secretary of the World Student Christian Federation, of which he was a founding father, embarking on a two-year world tour with the purpose of organising national student movements in India, China, Japan, Australia, New Zealand and Europe. Perhaps the leading promoter of the missionary cause, one of his books had the Watchword as its title, *The Evangelization of the World in this Generation*.

Bishop Stephen Neill observes that at the time of the Edinburgh conference, Mott was 45 and at the height of his powers. Although extremely focused on getting business done without distraction, and at times authoritarian in the chair, Neill has described him as 'firm, courteous and conciliatory', ensuring that every perspective had a fair airing.[31]

Here was a truly outstanding figure, a widely travelled and highly experienced international student leader and an eloquent and passionately committed exponent of the missionary imperative. Indeed, in Mott the fundamental link between the student and missionary movements of the time is personified.

One vital aspect of Mott's character was his global perspective. He was a strategist, one who knew the essential nature of planning and using the right people for the right tasks. He knew how to prioritise issues and could see what was of merely peripheral significance. Mott's guidance of the Edinburgh 1910 preparatory process had been an unqualified and indeed a phenomenal

---

30. While Mott was chairman, the President of the Conference was the Scottish peer and former British Cabinet minister, Lord Balfour of Burleigh.

31. S. Neill, *Men of Unity*, London: SCM, 1960, p 15

success; his own motto was: 'Plan as if there were no such thing as prayer. Pray as if there were no such thing as planning.'

Bishop Neill observes how Mott's work in the international student context had a direct bearing on the progress of Edinburgh 1910. The World Student Christian Federation embraced different Christian traditions and was a fellowship in which future leaders of church and state met; as the years passed, the significance of this would become ever clearer. A fundamental part of the rationale of student fellowship was the nurturing of faith in those who would be most influential in the affairs of the world.

The ideal of fellowship and co-operation across denominational lines was thus naturally a fundamental principle in the thinking that led to Edinburgh 1910, and in the conference itself. Neill writes: 'Many of the leaders in the preparations for the Edinburgh Conference had moved in Student Movement circles and were familiar with this new principle of co-operation. It was this that made possible the presence at the Conference of certain groups which, without the acceptance of this principle, would certainly not have been there.'[32] Among those who accepted the invitation to Edinburgh 1910 in the light of the new co-operative spirit, Neill asserts, was none other than the Archbishop of Canterbury, Randall Davidson. Born a Scottish Presbyterian, Davidson was confirmed into the Church of England while at school at Harrow, and his archiepiscopate is noted for his strength of leadership and his determination to uphold Anglican comprehensiveness. Yet his attendance at Edinburgh 1910 was not to be taken for granted; Ernest Payne has written of Davidson's initial hesitation about taking part in the gathering along with such a breadth of Protestant traditions, including Baptists and Congregationalists, and of the 'suspicious' approach of some representatives to one another – although this was not by any means to be a characteristic of the conference.[33] Bishop Charles Gore was one who epitomised Anglo-Catholicism and

32. Ibid., p 19
33. E. A. Payne, *Toleration and Establishment: 1 – A historical outline*, in Ed G. F. Nuttall and O. Chadwick, *From Uniformity to Unity: 1662-1962*, London: SPCK, 1962, p 286

his presence at Edinburgh 1910 can well be seen as having to a considerable degree enabled the Archbishop of Canterbury and other Anglican figures to participate in the conference, and indeed in the subsequent ecumenical movement.

Bishop James Mehaffey has written of 'sharp tension' that had arisen at the time between the Anglo-Catholic party in the Church of England and evangelicals in general on the subject of Christian unity. He writes: 'The Anglo-Catholics insisted on unity in truth. By truth they meant the acceptance of Anglican doctrine as they understood it and their own particular interpretation of the nature of the ministry and the sacraments, all based squarely on a somewhat rigid doctrine of apostolic succession.' He goes on to point out that while Anglo-Catholics believed that 'interdenominational' movements towards unity sacrificed truth for the sake of unity, evangelicals stressed the need for unity in fundamental aspects of doctrine but also the ideal of unity in fellowship.[34]

Edinburgh 1910 was thus not a gathering of the wholly like-minded in terms of missionary outlook or theology or churchmanship; rather, it was a gathering across such boundaries – low church and high church, episcopal and non-episcopal, liberal and conservative – with one common aim: evangelisation.

A rousing passage at the end of Chapter 2 in Mott's *The Evangelization of the World in this Generation*, published in 1899, captures his powerful eloquence, his sheer determination and the sense of missionary urgency at the time: 'Because of the infinite need of men without Christ; because of the possibilities of men of every race and condition who take Christ as the Lord of their lives; because of the command of our Lord which has acquired added force as a result of nineteen centuries of discovery, of opening doors, of experience of the Christian church; because of the shameful neglect of the past; because of the impending crisis and the urgency of the situation in all parts of the non-Christian world; because of the opportunity for a greatly accelerated movement in the present; because of the danger of neglecting to enter

---

34. J. Mehaffey, *The Development of the Idea of the Unity of the Church in Ecumenical Discussion from Edinburgh 1910 to New Delhi 1961*, QUB PhD thesis 1975, p 22

upon a great onward movement; because of the constraining memories of the cross of Christ and the love wherewith he loved us – it is the solemn duty of the Christians of this generation to do their utmost to evangelise the world.'[35]

While Mott was chairman of Edinburgh 1910, J. H. Oldham (1874-1969) was the general secretary. The former was an American, the latter a Scot, although born in India. The two contrasted also as personalities – Mott an imposing figure who would speak authoritatively, Oldham physically smaller and by nature of modest and quiet disposition, never actually addressing the conference except for routine notices.

J. H. Oldham had been secretary of the United Free Church of Scotland's Mission Study Council and study secretary of the Student Christian Movement. He was seconded by the SCM to be general secretary of Edinburgh 1910, following which he was permanently released to be secretary of Edinburgh 1910's continuation committee, from which in turn issued the prestigious journal, *The International Review of Missions,*[36] and the highly significant International Missionary Council of which he was elected secretary in 1911. In his earlier days, Oldham, as a student at Oxford, had been a leading figure in the Student Volunteer Movement in Britain and his involvement in Edinburgh 1910 was largely due to Mott's influence, who had identified him as the right person for the administrative job.

Not only had the preparatory process for Edinburgh 1910 been thorough, to say the least, but the actual attendance was a very highly distinguished gathering of 1,200 delegates from all over the world. It was truly a global gathering of mission leaders, although indigenous Christians of mission lands thereby were effectively sidelined. Gairdner records that mission boards and societies in all countries were entitled to send delegations in pro-

35. J. R. Mott, *The Evangelization of the World in this Generation,* SVMU, 1899. As in Tatlow, op. cit., p 112

36. In 1969, the name was changed to *The International Review of Mission* (singular). The Editorial of April 1969, by William H. Crane, indicated that the change was to reflect the fact that the mission of the church is one, and declared that the old title perpetuated a "host of outdated images" of mission.

portion to their income.[37] In addition, leading church administrators and clergy were present, as well as the most renowned missiologists and leaders in public life: US President Theodore Roosevelt was a named delegate of the Dutch Reformed Church of America who, unable to attend, sent a personal message to the conference. While the Orthodox and Roman Catholic churches were not represented, there was a broad spectrum of communions within the Protestant tradition and Gairdner, looking back on Edinburgh 1910, could look forward, however tentatively, to a more ecumenical future. He writes: 'The communions whose absence at once strikes the observer are of course the great Greek and Roman Churches – the former with its notable Japan mission, the latter (Church of Xavier yesterday and Lavigerie today) with foreign missions all over the world. But who, on this ridge of memories and of hopes, can say what the future may bring forth?'[38]

This was, of course, from today's perspective a huge deficiency, but there is an inherent inconsistency in applying the standards of one age to a much earlier one. Indeed, fully ecumenical mission is not even a straightforward issue today. So, there is great achievement to be acknowledged in the way in which Edinburgh 1910, given the circumstances of its day, brought together very diverse theological and ecclesiastical backgrounds. There can be no doubt that this was a definite advance which, in turn, prepared the way for greater co-operation between the churches and for the modern ecumenical movement itself.

In 1910 there was not yet any national council of churches; there was no formal ecumenical movement such as we are familiar with today. Orthodoxy and Protestantism were traditionally and culturally, even more so than today, at a remove from each other, and Rome was still a long way off from Vatican II. Yet the coming into the ecumenical mainstream of both Orthodoxy and the Roman Catholic Church is part of the unfolding modern ecumenical movement, of which Edinburgh 1910 was, in its own quite distinctive and dramatic way, a launching; to these happy

37. Gairdner, op. cit., pp 47f
38. Ibid., p 50

developments we shall come in due course. Moreover, K. S. Latourette has written of the *The International Review of Missions*, the first issue of which appeared in 1912: 'The Review immediately took its place as the outstanding supra-confessional international journal in the field of missions. Its wide range of contributors and reviewers, from many and differing ecclesiastical and theological traditions, its extensive bibliographies, and its annual surveys of the world mission, covering as they did Roman Catholic as well as Protestant developments, contributed notably to the nourishment of the ecumenical spirit.'[39]

In session, Edinburgh 1910 followed very closely to the agenda of the eight commission reports, to which reference has been made above and which we will consider in the next chapter of this book. Mott, in chairing the proceedings, held the delegates to that business with the diligence and single-mindedness that, no doubt, was only expected from him. The firmness, yet judiciousness and discernment of his temperament is clear in Gairdner's commentary on his speaking style: 'Every sentence is brought down like a blow; and, as when the heavy arm of some stone-breaker bangs blow on blow of the heart of a lump of stone, until it fairly smashes into fragments, not otherwise hammer the sentences of John R. Mott, with careful, scientific deliberateness, until, at the end, the audience finds itself, in a word – smashed … And then the tenderness of the man comes out – as he deals with the fragments.'[40] A chairman to be feared in a way, perhaps, but clearly also one who was most highly regarded.

Whatever about Mott's awesomeness, as a chairman he did not enter debate but simply chaired. He was not there to impose his will but to enable the will and direction of thought of the delegates to come to light. In any case, his style clearly did not hinder speakers from seeking the platform: because of time constraints, far from all those who wanted to address the gathering were able

---

39. K.S. Latourette, *Ecumenical Bearings of the Missionary Movement and the International Missionary Council*, Ch 8 in Ed R. Rouse and S. Neill, *A History of the Ecumenical Movement: 1517-1948*, London: SPCK, 1948, pp 363f. Latourette, a renowned missionary historian, was Professor of Missions at Yale University.
40. Gairdner, op. cit., p 64

to do so. Moreover, as may be envisaged from the make-up of the delegates, contributions to debate were consistently of a high calibre. Edinburgh 1910, marked in its worship – as Stanley observes – by a remarkable depth of prayer and meditation,[41] was indeed a serious and godly deliberation.

---

41. Op. cit., pp 88 and 90

CHAPTER TWO

The Business of the Conference

Edinburgh 1910, as mentioned in the previous chapter, was organised under eight themes. Preparatory commissions drew up reports which were circulated before the meeting, so that those coming to the conference would be well briefed before the topics were discussed in session. The work of these commissions was extensive and meticulous, with questionnaires being returned to the commissions from the mission field. Each of the eight themes was a huge topic in itself.

15 June: Carrying the gospel to all the non-Christian world
The first thing that is striking about the report of the commission under this topic is the sheer extent of the task. No doubt, coming to the conference, delegates had felt enthusiasm for the missionary challenge, but the report – some 300 pages – may well have tempered such feelings because while it recorded successes it also spelled out the very considerable difficulties being faced in the mission field.

When one considered the geographical and demographic size of Africa, for example, with huge tracts as yet unclaimed by either Christianity or Islam, other huge tracts already taken by Islam, and other huge tracts where the Christian mission was inadequate to meet the demands, there was cause to be deeply perturbed. Nonetheless, other reports from Africa showed missionary advance and success, such as in Nigeria or Uganda but, still, there was a mammoth challenge. And that was only Africa.

India was a heavily populated land where highly trained missionaries were needed, but they were not coming forward in the numbers that were required. The report of the commission noted: 'Apart from the Jewish people ... there is no great nation or group of nations except India, the whole life and being of which have been dominated by religious interests.' However, it stated baldly that the existing missionary effort in India was simply 'inadequate'. The report listed five groups which the Christian mission had to reach: (1) the 50 million of the outcastes and of the lowest castes; (2) the 160 million Hindus, belonging to a very varied religion; (3) the 60 million 'Mohammedans' who had generally been neglected by Christian missionaries in India; (4) the 10 million Buddhists; and (5) the one million English-speaking people of differing religious adherence. The challenge was summarised: 'The present hour is one of unprecedented opportunity. It is correspondingly one of tremendous responsibility for the church of Christ. The crucial question is, Will the church rise to its great task in India?'[1]

As for China, this was a time of opportunity for Christian missionary work but, again, the scale of the endeavour was daunting, although there were examples of successful missions. The commission's report noted that estimates of the total number of the population of China and its Empire varied from 350 to just over 433.5 million. However, statistics revealed between 38,000 and 332,000 people per missionary in the provinces, excluding the Roman Catholic missions. However, despite the need for more missionaries, some experienced missionary leaders in the field warned that the arrival of a large number 'would probably occasion governmental opposition, and call forth the antagonism of a numerous body of patriots who are fearful of foreign influence'.[2] Clearly, there were many factors to be taken into consideration in planning the future of the missionary effort in China.

As for Japan, the commission's report ventured to suggest that the 'age-long dominance of Buddhism has probably been more of a hindrance than a help to Christendom'. It had bred 'superstition, fatalism, and a low conception of sin and of salvation by faith', although it had also taught positive things, not least the need for 'spiritual enlightenment'.[3]

---

1. *Report of Commission I*, Edinburgh and London: Oliphant, Anderson & Ferrier, pp 135, 160, 147 and 163
2. Ibid., p 102
3. Ibid., p 52

Statistics showed church membership as having grown in Japan from 2,701 in 1879 to 73,422 in 1908; the Roman Catholic and Greek Catholic churches claimed 62,000 and 30,000 respectively. The report recorded a conservative consensus of opinion calling for an increase of 25 per cent of missionary leaders over the following ten years, with the desired increase in Japanese workers in mission being 'practically unlimited'.[4] These Japanese church workers would increasingly bear the burdens of the task.

It was noted that the evangelisation of Japan was not an isolated question, the nation's moral and intellectual influence already powerfully affecting China, Korea, Siam, India and even Turkey.[5] The evangelisation of Japan was thus seen to be vitally important from a missionary-strategic point of view.

In addition to these areas, there were some difficult and relatively much more inaccessible lands, as in central Asia. There was considerable sentiment against new missionary societies joining existing missions and not going forth into new regions; yet, on the other hand, there was also a sense that it was a good strategy to build on strengths so that new, native churches could become independent and then in turn themselves forward the mission of Christ.

The fact that there were very considerable areas of the world that were still 'unoccupied' – that is, not having been converted to any of the greater religions – was considered a reproach to the church. Here were delegates from voluntary missionary societies conferring on the evangelisation of the world, but where were their institutional churches in this endeavour?

Such an outlook could have created a cloud of gloom over the Edinburgh 1910 conference, but it did not do so. The meeting together and the hearing of real advances in certain parts of the world, of real commitment and heroism, and of new Christians in different lands taking on the missionary cause in exemplary ways, was of such inspiration that the difficulties were not allowed to dim the spirit.

The topic of this, the first of the commissions to report, naturally

4. Ibid., p 58
5. Ibid., p 166

led into other areas covered by commission reports that were to come later in the conference. This was particularly true when it came to considering how to respond to the vastness of the global missionary task and challenge. Clearly, a fundamental part of the approach had to lie in much greater co-ordination of effort on the part of the missionary societies. Vitally important here was the suggestion, already brought forward on the first day and to be a recurring topic, that a central co-ordinating body was needed, so that the missionary approach to the world would not be haphazard or unplanned, but clearly thought through and efficiently carried out.

Another topic that arose under the first commission's report, and which would recur, was the need for vibrancy and real commitment and growth in the church at home. The 'home base' had to be alive for Christ if it was to have the motivation, energy and determination to take up the unique missionary opportunity that all understood as presenting itself just at this time in history.

16 June: The Church in the Mission Field
In considering the report on the church in its missionary context, what is clear when one considers the matter quickly became apparent to the delegates assembled at Edinburgh 1910. That is, that the church in the 'mission field' was far from uniform in terms of its development and maturity. Some mission stations were in their infancy, others were nothing less that fully fledged congregations with effective pastoral and outreach ministries and established worship patterns. The church in its missionary context was seen to be extremely varied in terms of development of the Christian community. Indeed, as speaker followed speaker, it became clear that the young daughter churches in newly evangelised territories were so often vibrant and full of potential. There was a vitality there that inspired confidence in what could be achieved. It was heartening for the conference to be told of situations that bore witness to real spiritual energy and drive; moreover, it was reported that there were almost two million communicants registered across what were seen as the 'mission territories'.

Some congregations and churches were self-supporting, even

having their own polity in terms of constitutions and laws, and it was recognised that many more needed to be helped to achieve such independence and self-governance. It was felt by some speakers that the missionary societies and boards clung on to too much power for themselves and were too reluctant to help the new daughter churches become established in their own right and with their own distinctive character, identity and priorities.

Having surveyed the varying polities of the church in the mission field – including congregational, continental European, Anglican, Presbyterian, Methodist and interdenominational – the commission's report went on to indicate that it was the almost universally accepted missionary principle to assist self-government in mission churches, but making the transition 'from the elementary stage of dependence on a foreign mission to that of the self-support of the young church'[6] was a critical and far from straightforward issue, not least in terms of Christian teaching, discipline and general organisation.

There was, in fact, such a thing as the 'home mission' of these new congregations across Africa, Asia, South America and the Pacific as they reached out with missionary zeal that was, at times, truly remarkable. Yet, especially where advance had been rapid, it was recognised that there was a need to put resources in place to ensure proper nurturing and religious education of new Christians in their faith. Some concern was expressed at the conference that there was at times too much of a tendency to denominationalise the emergent churches, rather than to let them establish their own identities. Nonetheless, there can be no doubt that the delegates to Edinburgh 1910 must have been profoundly moved when they heard reports of real sacrifices being made by new converts in distant lands – sacrifices that included martyrdom itself.

The report of the commission on the church in the mission field pointed to real pastoral difficulties, such as dealing with local traditions of ancestor worship, caste or polygamy, but as Gairdner records, these topics did not figure particularly in discussion in conference session: 'Just twice they came to the surface, and each

---

6. *Report of Commission II*, p 35

time the exceptionally moved tone of the speaker's voice indicated the travail in which the church still is with these painfully difficult questions.'[7] He goes on to recall how a Japanese delegate pleaded for patience in dealing with the caste issue as, he believed, time was needed for the Indian church to realise the full significance of its faith.

The commission's report had itself made clear, for example, that polygamy was a sensitive issue, pointing out the considerations that had to be given to the protection of children and wives and that the woman 'put away finds herself, according to many letters before us, in the position of gravest moral danger'.[8] The report summarised the question as 'whether the heinousness of the sin of polygamy does not consist in the very fact that it is impossible to undo its results, without fresh violations of Christian righteousness'.[9]

The commission made it clear in its report that having engaged in an extensive survey of the church in the mission field, across denominational divides, the members of the commission had 'come to a clearer understanding of each other's principles and position, and rejoice to recognise that we can all learn from each other's teaching and polity, without being unfaithful to our own'.[10]

It is interesting to note, as Gairdner writes, how the discussion of this report pointed to deeper ecclesiological questions which in turn were addressed in debate by two Anglican bishops – Bishop Roots, of Hankow in China, and Bishop Gore, of Birmingham. Bishop Roots emphasised how missionaries should not leave China until such time as the Chinese church was able to sustain its relationship with the 'Universal Church', and Bishop Gore stressed the need to have a clear understanding of just what constitutes the church. Here we can see profound ecclesiological questions that still are the subject of live debate today and, in addressing them in however limited a way, the conference was al-

---

7. Gairdner, op. cit., p 102
8. *Report of Commission II*, p 65
9. Ibid., p 68
10. Ibid., p 266

ready anticipating some of the concerns of the subsequent faith and order movement. However, discussion of faith and order matters had been ruled out of Edinburgh 1910's brief, which was to remain focused on the more strategic aspect of missionary planning. Of course, had doctrinal matters been open to discussion by the delegates, the conference would have most probably have taken a wholly different direction and certainly, at least, time would have run out very quickly.

17 June: Education in relation to the Christianisation of National Life
There was a natural progression from the theme of 'The Church in the Mission Field' to this third topic, not least because it had become clear that if new, young churches in mission lands were to be built up and were to have any chance of maturing in their faith and worship, education was going to be vital. If there was to be effective pastoral leadership, it needed proper training and, indeed, training based on sound theology. Education is a fundamental priority for any nation seeking to build itself up or to maintain its position or to be secure as it faces the future; exactly the same applies to the church.

Yet under the theme of 'Education in relation to the Christianisation of National Life' it very quickly became clear that much more was at stake than ministerial training or theological education. If the mission lands were to become Christian lands, then the people were going to have to be educated in accordance with Christian principles – and this had a bearing on the totality of the educational curriculum. The relating of Christian truth in all its breadth of application to indigenous perspectives was a task that would require the utmost sensitivity and feeling. The report of the commission pointed out somewhat ominously, for example, that 'on the whole, singularly little attention has been paid to presenting Christianity in the form best suited to the Oriental spirit. The converts have been introduced to controversies and confessions purely western in character and phraseology.'[11]

There was no point in simply dismissing all indigenous ways as though they were worthless; the best approach would be one of

---

11. *Report of Commission III*, p. 245

true respect. The commission quoted the perspective of Dr D. Z. Sheffield on Christianity in China: 'Christian scholars who study the Confucian classics at first hand are usually surprised and always delight at the high ethical standards therein presented in political, social and individual life. The Christian teacher or preacher, if he is wise, will make himself familiar with those teachings, using them as lines of approach to the minds and hearts of the people.'[12]

Similarly, there was no point in gearing all educational work towards attaining western educational qualifications; a much greater place had to be given to the cultural context of the particular mission land and its demands. The Christian teacher, in imparting a Christian perspective in the whole compass of the educational programme, would have to do so with a sympathy for the existing culture, while seeking to move people on to a deeper knowledge of God through the Christian revelation. So, the task of missionary educators in the mission field, in seeking to 'Christianise' national life in the non-Christian mission lands, by developing and moulding a Christian awareness, was a particularly critical one.

The report of the commission noted how the replies to its questionnaire from the mission field had emphasised three points: the importance of training native leaders; the use of the vernacular in religious instruction; and the focusing on the fundamental elements of Christianity, not highlighting western divisions.

During the discussion at Edinburgh 1910 on the report of the commission on this theme, it became very clear that there was a great under-resourcing in terms of the supply of missionary teachers. The work of the commission had revealed that many of the same problems were found in nearly all parts of the missionary outreach throughout the world; in dealing with the 'Christianisation of national life', the commission had been constantly confronted with the problems that existed in finding competent Christian teachers, both men and women, but also stressed the importance of placing properly trained teachers, who were native to the relevant country, in positions of educational leader-

12. Ibid., p 249

ship and responsibility. The commission also stressed that 'in all
plans for Christian education, women ought to receive equal consideration with men'.[13]

It also became clear that, additionally, resources had to be directed towards providing higher education. The establishing of a
Christian university in Japan, of providing the highest standards
of education such as would attract the higher castes in India, and
of meeting the challenging intellectual needs of China, in fact
were very considerable demands in terms of financial and personnel resources. The problem here was not only the scale of the need
but was compounded by the fact that secular authorities were
willing to pay educators much more than the missionary societies
could afford. Why work for a mission when one could earn as
much as fifteen times the amount on offer doing the same educational or development work for the state? The answer could only
lie in commitment.

The credibility of the Christian mission, in particular in Japan,
India and China, in many ways would depend on the church
being intellectually capable. The commission's report indicated in
relation to the Chinese context: 'If Christianity does not speedily
develop an educated ministry, it will soon fail to command respect or exert any great influence over the people and their leaders. Everything lies within the grasp of Christianity now, if the
best talent of the native church can be given good Christian educational advantages.'[14]

The 'Christianising' of national life across the globe was an
enormous vision; a basic priority in this was the Christian education of those who were going to be of influence in leading the
nations forward to a more developed future. This meant that the
missionary societies would have to be in a position to impart
education that was more than elementary and that, in fact, was
able to reach the highest levels. That there were opportunities and
prospects for success could not be doubted, but even with the best
awareness of the need and the best organisation, the question remained as to where the individuals would come from to staff the

13. Ibid., p 377
14. Ibid., p 130

educational mission. Moreover, there also remained the question of finance. The commission commented that seldom had the Christian church been called 'to meet so great an opportunity, or to respond to such immense and varied needs', adding that if a worthy response was to be made to that call, both personnel and money 'must be given for the promotion of Christian education in far more abundant measure than has been done in the past'.[15]

Despite the insights of Edinburgh 1910 on this subject, Brian Stanley points out that the conference in fact led to the establishment of very few educational institutions. He continues: 'By 1931, many of the arguments advanced by Commission III were looking decidedly threadbare. For all of the theological creativity evinced by Moore, Burton and Gore in ensuring that the Commission took proper note of the need for indigenous expressions of Christianity, the report of Commission III is likely to be dismissed by most readers today as a document which failed to grasp the necessity of developing strategies of education for the non-western churches that would not in the long run impair their future growth towards self-sustaining life.'[16]

The difficulties in making a practical impact in the area of education were very clear at Edinburgh 1910, and subsequent lack of advance proved their depth and seriousness.

18 June: The Missionary Message in relation to Non-Christian religions
Edinburgh 1910 thought in terms of five major religious categories, outside Christianity: Animism, Chinese religions, Japanese religions, Islam and Hinduism. However, the mood of the conference was not such as to view the non-Christian religions as of no value at all; rather, they were seen as having differing values, with Christianity being, as it were, the crown. Coming out of the reports from the mission field there was an evident respect for other religions and a rejection of any outright dismissal of their intrinsic

---

15. Ibid., p 380
16. B. Stanley, *The World Missionary Conference, Edinburgh 1910*, op. cit., pp 200f. (Moore, Prof Edward C., vice-chairman of Commission III; Burton, Prof Ernest deWitt; Gore, Charles, Anglican Bishop of Birmingham and chairman of Commission III)

religious worth. The truth was seen as being in them, but the fullness of truth was to be found in the Christian revelation. Gairdner comments: 'And while of course theories as to the origin and significance of the non-Christian religions still vary, there is a general consensus that, representing as they do so many attempted solutions of life's problem, they must be approached with very real sympathy and respect …'[17]

Brian Stanley, having drawn attention to Kenneth Cracknell's view that Commission IV had expounded 'an 'incipient theology of dialogue' that combined a belief in the finality of the Christian revelation with a generous and humble attitude to the insights of other religious traditions', goes on to refer to many of Commission IV's respondents: 'All religious phenomena were placed somewhere along a scale of progression from the "lower" to the "higher" forms of religion. The Spirit of God was said to be at work in all such phenomena, though less obviously so at the lower points of the scale … The presumed future trajectory of world religions was still one of the replacement of all other religions by Christianity, but that replacement was conceived of as a gradual process of absorption rather than an abrupt one of confrontation.' Stanley also notes how J. S. Friesen, who has worked in particular on responses to Commission IV on the subject of 'primal' or 'animinst' religion, has asserted that 'the characterisation that missionaries at Edinburgh regarded African religions as demonic and to be uprooted is a judgement which is not supported by the research'. Stanley adds that, on the contrary, missionaries in primal contexts were engaged 'in a conversational process in the interreligious encounter and witness', in Friesen's view.[18]

What was needed, it was felt by those concerned in 1910, was sound understanding of the non-Christian religions, so that it might be possible to find points of contact through which to estab-

---

17. Gairdner, op. cit., p 137
18. Stanley, op. cit., pp 206f; K. Cracknell, *Justice, Courtesy and Love: theologians and missionaries encountering world religions, 1846-1914*, London: Epworth Press, 1995, pp 194, 202, 259-60.; Stanley, op. cit., pp 246 and 207, respectively; J. S. Friesen, *Missionary Responses to Tribal Religions at Edinburgh, 1910*, New York: Peter Lang, 1996, p 141

lish some fruitful discussion as a way of pointing others to the
truth of Christ. The light of the world being Christ, other religions
were seen as 'broken lights', or as lights that could only reveal part
of the truth. Yet this insight in itself posed a real challenge to the
church and its faith: if Christ is the one true light, does the church
really live in that light and does the church really shine that light
in the world, even in Christian lands?

The need to understand others in order to be able effectively to
present them with Christianity was clearly understood at the
Edinburgh conference; the finding of points of contact and, moreover, the willingness to find examples in others displayed an
openness that is perhaps in some ways unexpected. A key factor
in the development of such an approach was undoubtedly the fact
that the conference was listening very closely to the voices of missionaries themselves, through the reports they had sent and
which formed the bases of the eight commissions' reports. This
was no purely theoretical exercise, no 'ivory tower' enterprise;
rather, Edinburgh 1910 was rooted and grounded in the actual experience of serving missionaries. Their insights were the basis for
the further deliberation on the conference floor.

A striking conclusion was reached regarding animism, a religious type that attaches significant powers to departed souls and
other spirit forms, and indeed includes a view of animals and natural life as having souls. Johannes Warneck (1864-1944), a
German theologian and son of the renowned missiologist, Gustav
Warneck, made the point that many of the fundamental theological claims of Christianity can appeal to the animist mind because
it is so confused: Christianity's one God, compared with the mult-
itude of spirits with which the animist has to contend;
Christianity's doctrine of salvation, compared with the complex
methods in which animists trusted in seeking reconciliation with
the higher powers; Christianity's concept of the resurrection of
the body, compared with the shadowy world of the spirits. For
Warneck, Christianity could present itself to animist people with
a real appeal, and he equally could point out: 'The animistic religions present certain points of contact for the preaching of the
gospel. Remnants of the conception of God are strong enough to

offer a basis for the new doctrine. The heathen sacrifices give a splendid opportunity for explaining Christian ideas, as do their disappointed prayers, which betray a need of the soul to grasp something beyond this world.'[19]

Turning to the matter of Chinese religion, animism was seen as lying at the root of its various expressions, and even at the basis of the moral compass of Confucianism. Yet it was observed that animism did not appear to have a credible future in China, given the fact that its thought categories were not in favour in Chinese schools, where non-religious and purely scientific understandings of life were predominating. In such a massive religious and spiritual vacuum, Christianity was seen to have a unique opportunity.

What was true of China was also true of Japan, where the distinctive characteristics of Christian morality and family life were understood to have a special attraction. However, what was seeming to hinder the wider appeal of Christianity to the people of Japan was the weakness of the church in the western world itself. If the Christian religion could not capture the people of its own lands, it was to be questioned.

As far as Buddhism was concerned, the commission could see certain connections with Christianity, in terms of spirituality, but it was not clear how truly satisfying Hinduism was; there was a connection point, and at this point Christianity had something of greater substance to give.

Equally, the connection between Islam and Christianity was clear in the common faith of a personal God, but the immense success of Islam posed direct questions and challenges to the churches in terms of the effectiveness of their mission and, indeed, the strength of their faith.

The commission's report stated: 'Islam presents a difficulty offered by no other religion. It cannot be regarded as anticipation, however defective, of the Christian gospel … It is not only later in point of time, but has also borrowed from Christianity as well as from Judaism …' Yet it was believed that emphasis should be

---

19. *Report of Commission IV*, p 22

placed on the common features of Christianity and Islam, while pointing out how 'these common features are found in a truer form in Christianity than in Islam.'[20]

Strikingly, the commission reported that statements by Muslim converts to Christianity showed that the person of Jesus was felt to be neither eastern nor western, but 'as universal as is man's need of him'.[21]

20 June: Relation of Missions to Governments
To consider the issue of relations between missionary societies and national governments was a considerable brief, not only because of the number of countries in which missionary work was in progress but also on account of the varying approaches of different governments to Christian missionary projects. This was by no means a uniform matter, any more than it is a uniform matter today. It also was noted at Edinburgh 1910 that there was no consensus on the issue of church-state relations as such. So, this commission's report revealed a considerable diversity of approaches and in actual relationships between mission projects, missionary societies and individual governments around the world. In fact, the great breadth of the matter served to underline the call at Edinburgh 1910 for an international missionary board of such standing that it would be able effectively to make representations to governments when necessary.

The commission's report, in illustrating the diversity of relations between governments and missionaries, stated: 'In Japan, for example, a fully civilised native government rules over a civilised and yet non-Christian people; in its neighbour, China, the government is both antiquated in methods and defective in policy, according to European standards ... in India a foreign Christian government controls the destinies of 300,000,000 Hindus and Mohammedans; in Mohammedan lands the law of Islam ... absolutely prohibits conversion to Christianity ... and in barbarian lands, still independent, the caprice of the chiefs, checked only by ancient usage and hereditary superstition, modi-

---

20. Ibid., p 140f
21. Ibid., p 154

fies the relations between them and the missionaries day by day.'[22]

The correspondence which the commission had received on this topic from missionaries in the mission field revealed that the work carried out by missionaries was being increasingly appreciated by governments and, indeed, in so far as they assisted towards national development, they were often seen as invaluable partners with governments. Brian Stanley has written: '[The] picture of growing harmony between missions and governments had some basis in fact. The General Acts of the Berlin Conference of 1884-85 and the Brussels Conference of 1890 had committed the European powers, albeit in vague terms, to the support of missions as part of a wider programme for the civilisation of Africa. Now that colonial frontiers were largely settled, missionaries seemed more frequently an asset than a threat.'[23]

A particular and interesting exception to this emerged. The characteristically secular policies of the French government also applied to the French colonies, with the result that those colonies were often very poorly evangelised or not really open to evangelisation. By contrast, the German government had a strikingly positive attitude to Christian missions, as had the Dutch. The German government actually sent a formal message to Edinburgh 1910: 'The German Colonial Office is following the proceedings of this World Missionary Conference with lively interest, and desires that it be crowned with blessing and success. The German Colonial Office recognises with satisfaction and gratitude that the endeavours for the spread of the gospel are followed by the blessings of civilisation and culture in all countries. In this sense, too, the good wishes of the Secretary of State of the German Imperial Colonial Office accompany your proceedings.'

The practice in the Dutch East Indies was particularly advanced in nature, the post of Missionary Consul having been established as a formal contact between missionaries there and the government.

---

22. *Report of Commission VII*, p 3
23. In ed A. Porter, *The Imperial Horizons on British Protestant Missions 1880-1914*, Grand Rapids and Cambridge: Eerdmans, 2003, p 74

Then again, the situation in Uganda was particularly encouraging. The commission's report recorded: 'The case of Uganda is in many ways unique. Without losing its national character, it has passed swiftly through the stages from untouched heathenism and independence to a dominant Christianity and European suzerainty. Only one Protestant mission has been at work in Uganda [The Church Mission(ary) Society], and it has exercised an enormous influence in shaping the destinies of the people and the actual political situation.'

If there were positive things to report and on which to reflect at Edinburgh, there were also developments that were the opposite, some very much so. The missionary situation in Sudan was a cause for despondency and concern, especially when it was reported that a Christian college had been converted into an Islamic one and that a Sudanese government official had indicated to Christians that 'You might as well give it up because we make ten Mohammedans to your one Christian.' Then again, in Northern Nigeria it was apparent that the government was favouring Islam. Worse still, there were some countries where Christian missionary work was not permitted at all (such as Nepal and Afghanistan), and in Turkey there was only nominal religious freedom, not least in so far as individuals were not allowed to convert.

The commission reported on Turkey: 'The convert from Islam takes his life in his hands. If public execution for apostasy is impossible, no limit can be put to the persecution which, privately or on false charges, he may have to endure. His only safety lies in flight.'[24] In Turkey, it was reported, mission work was definitely being hampered by the suspicions of the authorities.

It was reported that the only real sense of anger shown at Edinburgh 1910 was over three particular 'national wrongs': opium traffic, liquor traffic and enforced labour – also three subjects touched on by the then Archbishop of York in a special address at the conference. These matters were of concern to the missionary conference because of the inherent lack of moral rectitude. The opium trade in China was described as 'sinister and sordid'; as far

24. *Report of Commission VII*, p 47

as the liquor trade was concerned, there were reports of court fines and fees being paid in British Southern Nigeria with quantities of gin; in the Congo, taxes were being paid with forced labour and benefit in kind in rubber. The Congolese situation was particularly dire, with those failing to pay taxes as required facing unspeakable violence; because of the brutality associated with King Leopold II of Belgium's personal control over the Congo,[25] his colony, there was international pressure for control to pass to the Belgian parliament, which it did in 1908, leading to a considerable improvement in circumstances.

Andrew Porter writes that his review of thinking and activity in what is often regarded as 'the high imperial era' has suggested 'that missions' relationship with empire and its agents had lost nothing of its ambiguity' and certainly such a sense of ambiguity on this topic emerges from the Edinburgh 1910 experience. Porter perceptively comments: 'The internationalism of the missionary movement and its dynamics tended increasingly to separate national ambitions for empire and the global pursuit or fulfilment of evangelical goals.'[26]

The discussion on the report of the commission on missions and governments provided a comprehensive survey of situations around the globe, and the call for greater co-ordination of effort was a clear conclusion. Brian Stanley has commented, however, that it is difficult to establish the extent to which this report actually shaped subsequent relations between missions and governments; there were, indeed, few actual recommendations.[27] Nonetheless, it had become evident that there was an urgent need for a central body that could continue to survey developing situations in different parts of the world, with the ability and authority to act on behalf of missions in relating to governments. Without such a body, the missionary societies, mission stations and young churches would be left too much at the mercy of governments, un-

---

25. Leopold II, 1835-1909
26. A. Porter, *Religion versus empire? British Protestant missionaries and overseas expansion, 1700-1914*, Manchester University Press, 2005, pp 314f
27. A. Porter, *The Imperial Horizons on British Protestant Missions 1880-1914*, op. cit., p 78

able to make effective objections to unwelcome and disadvantageous policies.

21 June: Co-operation and the Promotion of Unity
Bishop Oliver Tomkins, while writing that the planners of Edinburgh 1910 had ruled out doctrinal discussions and 'reunion' talks, goes on to say: 'Yet it was theologically inevitable that to take seriously the church as apostolic led to the discovery of the call of the church to be one.'[28]

The report of the commission on co-operation and the promotion of unity, and the discussion at the conference, can only be described as of historic significance in this regard. It is not an overstatement to make such a observation. The commission's report could point out that the 'facts' showed how throughout the mission field there was a growing desire for the healing of the broken unity of the church. The objective, it was stated, should be 'to plant in every non-Christian nation one united church of Christ'.[29] Reflection on this aspect of Edinburgh 1910 makes it abundantly clear why the conference is regarded as the starting point of the modern ecumenical movement.

The Roman Catholic Church stood apart from the conference, and the commission's report indicated: 'The statements in the following pages do not include any reference to co-operation with Roman Catholics. The evidence before the Commission shows that, while in many mission fields personal relations with Roman Catholic missionaries are often of a friendly character, and individual acts of courtesy are not uncommon, the representatives of the Roman Catholic Church hold themselves precluded from entering into any agreement or taking part in any practical effort with the representatives of other Christian bodies.'[30]

The proceedings during the day devoted to this subject commenced with reports on co-operation as it is practised in the mission field. The commission's report had made it clear how de-

---

28. O. Tomkins, *The Wholeness of the Church*, London: SCM, 1949, p 43, as in J. Mehaffey, op. cit., p 27
29. *Report of Commission VIII*, p 131
30. Ibid., p 3

sirable it was felt to be that missions working in the same area should agree on a common plan in order to advance their common cause with greatest effectiveness, avoiding overlapping and a consequent waste of effort. Moreover, it made a very strong appeal that no missionary society should commence work in a particular area without first consulting any other missions operating in the area and seeking to find an understanding with them.

There was also a very practical purpose behind greater unity, as the commission explained: 'The resources provided by the church are so limited that it is essential, not only to press for additional forces, but also to employ to the utmost advantage the forces we have.' The following examples were given: arts colleges, medical colleges, higher education colleges, theological colleges (as far as possible), the school curriculum, Christian literature and mission presses.[31]

The situation in the mission field was, of course, the obvious place to start on this topic, but it quickly led beyond the matter of co-operation and into the theme of unity. The very progressive experience in China was of particular significance in bringing about this deepening of perspective. In western China there was a missionary advisory board, a clear understanding that missionary societies should not over-lap in the regions in which they operated, a common educational policy for mission schools, a united university, a common mission press, a common hymnbook and a church union committee. The issue of church unity in the mission field itself came to the fore; particularly when it came to the population's mobility, it was important that converts to Christianity should be able to associate fully with churches in different parts of the country. It became clear that feelings about the need for actual church union could lead the new church in China to go its own way, because it was obvious that there simply was no stomach for importing denominationalism.

Speaking at the conference, the Rev. E. W. Burt of the Baptist Mission in Shantung, north China, pointed to the more progressive spirit in the most recently entered mission fields when he commented: 'It is not enough to pay lip-service to the cause of

---

31. Ibid., pp 141f

unity ... I do not think that the principles of comity and unity have gone so far in any part as in West China. West China is one of the most recent fields to be entered, and it is in the recent fields that the spirit of comity is expressed today. It is in the older fields that we find most overlapping and most trouble.'[32]

Although such developments were not exclusive to China, there is no doubt that the Chinese experience was the leading progressive example. Gairdner refers to a striking speech at the conference by the Chinese delegate Cheng Ching-yi, which included the following words: 'The Christian federation movement occupies a chief place in the hearts of our leading Christian men in China, and they welcome every effort that is made towards that end. This is noticeably in the provinces of Szchuen, Honan, Shantung and Chihli. In educational work, evangelistic work, and so on, the churches joined hand in hand, and the result of this is most encouraging. Since the Chinese Christians have enjoyed the sweetness of such a unity, they long for more and look for yet greater things. They are watching with keen eyes, and listening with attentive ears, for what this Conference will show and say to them concerning this all-important question. I am sure they will not be disappointed. Speaking plainly, we hope to see in the near future a united Christian church without any denominational distinctions.'[33]

The challenge was clear, and it was coming from a young church that had enormous potential and that simply was unwilling to allow the advance of the gospel to be hindered by division in the church. Not only was the challenge clear, but so also was the rightness of the principle. The case was compelling.

Because of the undeniable significance of such perspectives being reported, a vast agenda opened up and so the day's proceedings moved towards the consideration of the creation of a continuation committee of Edinburgh 1910. This was not a 'set-up-a-committee' fudge, but was an earnest initiative to move the church and its mission forward.

The proposal that came to the conference from the commission

32. Ibid., p 192
33. Gairdner, op. cit., pp 184f

saw the continuation committee as taking responsibility for the future of such world missionary conferences and for the completion of any unfinished business of Edinburgh 1910. The envisaged continuation committee was to negotiate with mission societies and boards regarding the establishment of an International Missionary Committee. Such a committee was quite a different concept from the continuation committee, for an International Missionary Committee, if it were to co-ordinate world missionary endeavour, would have to be more directly appointed, and also approved, by the missionary boards and societies themselves. It could then replace the continuation committee, taking on its interest in the world missionary conference concept.

It is striking that the proposal for a continuation committee expressly stated that its concerns would not include the discussion of 'organic and ecclesiastical union'. This, no doubt, was due to the fact that such an agenda would be overwhelming and could distract the committee from its primary function, which was to see to the establishment of worldwide co-ordination of missionary work through an International Missionary Committee. It could also be contentious in itself, as there were differing views on what church unity actually meant. Nonetheless, the matter of church union was never far away at Edinburgh 1910, as we have already seen. Indeed, the brief of the commission embraced 'co-operation and the promotion of unity'. It is evident that by the end of the debate on the establishing of a continuation committee, although its terms of reference were limited as just indicated, there was a definite sense that this was leading into whole new territory – what would, in fact, become the churches' faith and order agenda. Gairdner indicates that the concept of a continuation committee, evolving into an International Missionary Committee , 'led the minds of the whole Conference to contemplate the vision of a higher unity still'; the continuation committee 'seemed to become transmuted by some sort of spiritual alchemy into a symbol of something greater far'.[34] Indeed, a lengthy letter read to the conference from the Roman Catholic Bishop Bonomelli, almost 80 years of age and reputed to have been a personal friend of the

---

34. Ibid., pp 195f

Pope, was striking for the sincerity of its good wishes and its truly ecumenical vision. It ended with these words: 'On this common ground, gentlemen, having your minds liberated from all passions or sectarian intolerance, animated, on the contrary, by Christian charity, bring together into one focus the results of your studies, the teachings of experience, whether individual or collective, calmly carry on research, and promote discussion. May truth be as a shining light, illuminating your consciences, and making you all of one heart and one mind. My desire for you is but the echo of Christ's words, which have resounded through the centuries: "Let there be one flock and one Shepherd".'[35]

The Irish Presbyterian minister, the Rev. R. K. Hanna, then of Whiteabbey, Co Antrim, included comments on the discussion of church unity in his reflections on Edinburgh 1910, at which he had been a delegate. He writes: 'A difference of view began, however, to manifest itself in the Conference as to how far this unity should be carried.' While there had been voices in favour of including the Roman Catholic Church in the vision of church unity, it was 'quite evident that these sentiments did not commend themselves to the vast majority of the delegates', Hanna writes, adding that it spoke much for the Christian forbearance that no formal protest was offered on the floor of the house. There had, however, been a rousing affirmation of an American speaker who declared: 'We are not prepared as American Christians to apologise for the Protestant religion.' Nonetheless, Hanna comments that this discussion at Edinburgh did good, having 'cleared the air', each side on the issue having stated its position and having heard the other.[36]

22 June: The Preparation of Missionaries

The report of the commission on the training of teachers and preparation of missionaries was detailed and comprehensive, yet while it identified areas that needed action, a major problem was

35. Ibid., pp 212f
36. R. K. Hanna, *The World Missionary Conference: Some impressions*, Belfast: Carswell, 1910, pp 20f (A copy of this 44-page booklet is held at the Gamble Library of Union Theological College, Belfast, ref. PAM-191-25)

the fact that Edinburgh 1910 was not a body to make executive decisions. Moreover, as Gairdner points out, those delegates at the
conference who were representing missionary boards or societies
or colleges were hesitant to commit themselves, or their institutions, to particular changes.[37] That was not their brief and they
would certainly have been overstepping their authority if they
tried to reach some agreed change of policy.

Nonetheless, the commission's report was a very significant
document because it was based precisely on extensive enquiries
to, and submissions from, such institutions as have been mentioned, as well as the mission field. It focused on the situation in
the mission field, the positive and negative aspects of the work of
the missionary institutions, and principles of training. So, while
not in a position to make any changes to the patterns of missionary
training, the conference could consider the situation and, indeed,
recognise where change was needed.

A fundamental issue was the recognition that the term 'missionary' itself was a very wide one; the report of the commission
held that it should be taken in its widest sense – ordained missionaries, medical missionaries, educationalists, nurses, teachers,
Bible readers, pastoral visitors, etc. Then again, as the Rev. Dr
Alexander Camphor of the Methodist Episcopal Church, USA
pointed out during the conference, there was a huge variety in the
contexts to which missionaries were sent and therefore the same
kind of training was not appropriate for all. Further, the missionary societies varied greatly in their capacities and motivation.
While missionary societies generally had high standards of
qualification for missionaries, not all societies met those standards.

Reports from the mission field revealed that while missionaries went forth into the mission lands with every dedication and
good intention, they often could find themselves unable to face
the immense challenges, not least from people who adhered very
strongly to whatever religion they already followed. The strength
of people's religious convictions and the natural tendency not to
want to depart from a religious tradition in which one has been

37. Gairdner, op. cit., p 217

nurtured from childhood made the task of seeking conversions extremely difficult and, in fact, demanding of great courage. For this task – the task of communicating the Christian gospel to people of well established religions – many missionaries simply were not adequately prepared, so that coping was a true challenge.

A question that came to the fore was whether, with such a perspective, one could be overstating the need. But this revealed only a tendency to deny the truth. Sending well intentioned people, no doubt endowed with ample common sense, was simply not good enough to meet the need. The training that was required, however, was not purely theoretical, but also practical and spiritual. So, missionaries needed to be competent – not necessarily great academics – and they needed to be able to relate to ordinary people and understand their predicaments. This was 'the commonplace missionary'.

It became clear in the discussion on this subject that there was, in fact, a very wide range of subjects that could all claim to be necessary in the process of missionary training. However, the commission's report identified five key areas.

First, the study of comparative religion was necessary because, self-evidently, the missionary was going to encounter other faiths and, if he or she was to communicate the gospel in any serious way, an understanding of the other's religion was essential. This was true not least in order to find points of contact between that religion and the Christian faith, on which the missionary could build in teaching and expounding Christ. The significance of this had, of course, already become clear to the conference in its discussion of the reports of the commissions on carrying the gospel to all the non-Christian world and the missionary message in relation to non-Christian religions.

Second, the missionary would need to be educated in the science and history of missions. Despite the extremely wide nature of missionary contexts, certain principles of missionary work were always applicable – such as the value to be accorded to non-Christian faiths. Then again, the understanding of missionary history would serve to help the missionary to learn from mistakes in the past; that is always vital, because nothing wastes both time and effort more than making the same mistakes over and over again and never learning from experience. The study of the history of missions would also help the missionary movement to see the way forward, to look to the future.

Third, the study of sociology was identified as important, although perhaps this might have been better described as anthropology – the study of the social life of other nations, indeed varying within particular nations, and the study of social movements in different societies. This understanding was seen as important because the task of the missionary was not to change foreign societies into the western mould, but to bring the gospel to those societies with their own social integrities.[38]

Fourth, pedagogy was stressed because so much of the missionary's work involved teaching; the understanding of teaching methods was therefore of fundamental importance. One of the striking things about this particular discussion was the participation of women delegates who, up until then in the conference, had not come to the fore. Gairdner notes that their participation in this debate made up for that by the quality of their addresses on this topic. Miss Jane Latham, who until recently had been principal of a London missionary training college, pointed out that pedagogical instruction was important not least because one of the frequent tasks of missionaries was, quite simply, to teach how to teach.[39]

Fifth, language study was obviously essential. However, the truth of the matter was that this was not being done very effectively, with language syllabuses that were both inadequate and dated.

During discussion at the conference, Miss Belle Bennett from the Women's Foreign Missionary Society of the Methodist Episcopal Church, USA called for training institutions to be located in the mission field, allied to preparatory study at home. In this way, she held, those being trained would gain a better understanding of local customs and religion.[40]

What became clear in all of this was, once again, the immense value that would result from co-operation among missionary so-

---

38. *Report of Commission V*, p 230
39. Ibid., pp 224, 231
40. Ibid., p 312

cieties and institutions. Duplication was only wasteful of already scarce resources. So, this clearly was a matter for the intended continuation committee to address. The commission had already made the point: 'The need for a body definitely commissioned to examine into and co-ordinate the possibilities for special missionary preparation has led the Commission to propose that steps should be taken by the World Missionary Conference to secure the creation of a permanent Board of Missionary Study by the joint action of the different Societies and Boards.'[41]

The words of a Miss Humphrey, who was a member of an Anglican Candidates' committee, made the point vividly: 'Why should each society go on throwing up its little molehill of knowledge and experience in such things, when we might all contribute to raise a great mountain of wisdom – for the benefit of all, as well as of each? And in the meantime, I, for one, go away from this Conference, fully purposing to try whether those of us in Great Britain, who are interested in the selection and training of women-missionaries, cannot meet informally in the autumn to confer as to the possibility of common action in certain matters as a beginning.'[42]

Women in the Missionary Movement

The issue of women's participation in the Protestant missionary endeavour has become clear in this section of our consideration of Edinburgh 1910. Deborah Gaitskell, in a recent study of the subject, has pointed out that by the early twentieth century, and as a result of a great increase in the recruitment of women to missionary work, women in fact outnumbered men in the mission field. She adds that it is broadly the case that until the separate women's missionary societies were up and running, the deployment of British Protestant women was restricted to wives, 'married to the job' – and often married *for* the job.[43]

Gaitskell continues: 'By 1900, of 18,782 missionaries throughout the world, 3,628 were single women and 4,340 wives; by 1929

41. Ibid., p 210
42. Ibid., p 233
43. D. Gaitskell, *Rethinking Gender Roles: The Field Experience of Women Missionaries in South Africa*, in ed. A. Porter, op. cit., p 133

two-thirds of the mission personnel of six US societies were female. Twin pressures proved decisive: "the needs of missionaries
abroad, and the aspirations of women at home". Missions argued
that the lack of female appointees had limited their success with
indigenous women; it simultaneously became clear that a fair
number of women wanted to go and a large number were prepared to form their own women's societies to fund and send
them.' She adds that British women's role in philanthropy and
much church work had been expanding, with feminists helping to
open up new opportunities in girls' education and teaching ca-
reers for women.[44]

Gaitskell's research into the situation in South Africa points to
the isolation and actual danger in which the first rural mission
wives lived, 'giving birth to perhaps ten children, far from medical help, feeding and clothing their families (and often a wider
household or community too) only through hard, time-consum-
ing effort, and squeezing in domestic and religious instruction for
local women and children intermittently and with difficulty – a
tale which can be replicated across the mission world'. Indeed,
Gaitskell comments that in 'supposedly healthy South Africa',
missionary wives faced many illnesses and suffered a considerable childbearing mortality rate.[45]

However, separate women's missionary societies came under
increasing pressure to surrender their autonomy; Brian Stanley
concludes that Edinburgh 1910 contributed to their decline, despite the fact that 'women themselves were consistently opposed
to the mergers with the male-dominated societies which took
place'.[46]

Patricia Grimshaw and Peter Sherlock have also researched
the subject of missionary women at the turn of the nineteenth and
twentieth centuries and note that the resources for the subject over
the last 200 years are 'diverse and dispersed, reflecting the wide
variety of experience depending on marital status, age, personal

---

44. Ibid., p 142
45. Ibid., pp 134 and 140f
46. B. Stanley, *The World Missionary Conference, Edinburgh 1910*, op. cit.,
p 315

capacity, and the possibilities for women's work offered by different denominations'. Noting how in 1907 the British schoolmaster,
Charles Hayward, had written on 'missionary heroines' as examples for the church at large, they assert that Hayward's collection
had been designed to show how women 'worked heroically until
old age or death, converting, educating and ministering to the
bodily needs of non-Christian people the world over'.[47]

Nonetheless, Grimshaw and Sherlock go on to raise the question of the extent to which women missionaries, despite all their
piety and sacrifices, were in fact complicit with men in terms of
Empire building: 'Since the late 1980s feminist scholars have been
forced to respond to post-colonial critiques questioning the role of
white women as agents of mission enterprises. Were women's
historians bent on discovering white women's significance in
Empire-building to valorise their roles? Should they not instead
be engaged in teasing out white women's complicity with white
men in sustaining colonial power structures at the expense of indigenous people?'[48] The question suggests an affirmative answer,
but the perspective here appears not to do justice to the complexity
of the motivations for missionary service nor indeed does it take
into account the ambiguous nature of the relationship between
missionary and imperial concerns such as has been referred to by
Andrew Porter.[49]

23 June: The Home Base of Missions
The final day of the 1910 Edinburgh Missionary Conference was
given over to the subject of the church 'at home', the sending
church. The ability of the church to communicate the gospel
throughout the world depends very fundamentally on its spiritual
state; it was necessary therefore that close consideration should
be given to this topic, vast though it undoubtedly was. Indeed, the

---

47. P. Grimshaw & P. Sherlock, *Women and Cultural Exchanges, in*
Missions and Empire, ed N. Etherington, Oxford University Press, Oxford
History of the British Empire, Companion Series, 2005, p 174
48. Ibid., p 177f
49. A. Porter, *Religion versus empire? British Protestant missionaries and*
overseas expansion, 1700-1914, Manchester University Press, 2005, p 314

report of the commission on this theme pointed out: 'It is evident that this problem is not one of machinery, but of life.'[50]

Prayer, the dissemination of literature, mission study classes, instruction on mission in educational institutions, visits to the mission field, and the Student Volunteer Movement all were topics raised in the commission's report. In fact, the conference was reminded by the report that mission visits abroad were greatly appreciated by the missions themselves: 'A fortnight's visit from one who is keenly interested in missions is one of the greatest tonics a mission can receive. The whole mission is refreshed by such a visit; helpful suggestions are made and permanent links are formed.'[51]

There were so many dimensions to the question of the church's spiritual state, not least the quality of ministerial training, the commitment of clergy in parishes to their vocation, the commitment of lay people to their faith, and the seriousness with which the church took the missionary calling. Then again, the ability of the church to rise to the great challenge depended to a large extent on its financial resources.

There was no doubt that in all of these areas and more there was immense scope for improvement; things were not as they could be or, in many cases, as they should be. The conference heard how the 'base of faith' was often weak, how actual giving to the church far from matched the potential, and how the church was not sufficiently missionary-minded.

The future of the church, as always, lay with young people, but the surveys carried out for the commission dealing with this topic found that work with young people was simply not sufficiently developed, and that nor was there an awareness of their actual needs. Referring to the securing of missionary volunteers, Gairdner writes: 'The consideration of this branch of the Home Base of Missions once again directed the minds of the delegates to the high, ultimate, inescapable question – the standard of Christian life in the church. It is surely the lowness of that standard which, in the last analysis, is accountable for the mass intel-

---

50. *Report of Commission VI*, p 6
51. Ibid., p 100

lectual unsettlement that exists among the students of the West.'[52] By contrast, Gairdner points to the vital role of women in the church and to the work done by women in the organisation of the conference itself and in the commissions.[53]

The commission's report had noted that over the previous fifty years, denominational and inter-denominational women's missionary societies or boards had greatly increased in number, both in the United States and in Europe, noting that at that time there were over sixty in active operation.[54] Women's missionary societies were connected to nearly all the regular denominational missionary societies and, as already noted, the question of integrating these was being raised; a problem was that of the duplication of missionary appeals and general administration. The commission concluded that decisions about this had to be left with each denomination; its own view was diplomatically put as being 'sympathetic to closer working'.[55]

Certainly by Gairdner's account, there was much lacking in the home base and the challenge facing the church in terms of its renewal and the stimulation of missionary zeal was daunting. In some ways, this was a rather inauspicious ending to the conference, but at least the delegates left with their feet on the ground.

The conference issued two messages – one to the members of the church in Christian lands and the other to those in non-Christian lands.

The message of the conference to the church in Christian lands emphasised the sense of a time of great opportunity for the church in the work of world evangelisation and saw the coming ten years as crucial in that endeavour, a 'kairos' moment in the history of the church. 'If those years are wasted, havoc may be wrought that centuries are not able to repair. On the other hand, if they are rightly used they may be among the most glorious in Christian history.' What was now needed was a much deeper sense,

---

52. Gairdner, op. cit., p 247
53. Ibid., p 252
54. *Report of Commission VI*, p 223
55. Ibid., p 234

throughout the church, of its responsibility before God. The grace of God was needed, and had to be sought.

Addressing the church in non-Christian lands, the conference spoke of the energy of the young church in so many different contexts around the world: 'Many cases of thanksgiving have arisen as we have consulted together, with the whole of the Mission Field clear in view. But nothing has caused more joy than the witness borne from all quarters as to the steady growth in numbers, zeal, and power of the rising Christian church in newly-awakening lands.'

What made this sense of the vitality of the rising church all the more inspiring was the fact that it faced many and great difficulties. These had become clear as the conference had progressed and as the reports from the mission field had been considered in the material before the conference. The challenge of bringing the good news of the gospel to people of other established faiths and in lands where Christians faced persecution was being met by new Christians who showed not only spiritual strength but also real courage. This was, truly, an inspiration for the conference and provided real hope for the future.

The conference closed with the moving words of its chairman, John R. Mott, that 'though there have been few resolutions, though there have been no signs and sounds and wonders as of the rushing wind, God has been silently and peacefully doing his work'.[56]

---

56. *History and Records*, Vol. IX, p 347

CHAPTER THREE

The Fruits of Edinburgh 1910

The Edinburgh Missionary Conference of 1910 not only led to further work in terms of co-ordination of the missionary endeavour by the conference's continuation committee and, eventually, the new International Missionary Council, but also gave rise to two further movements: faith and order, and life and work. The former focused on doctrinal discussions among the churches and the latter focused on their more social and political responsibilities. Taken together, the three broad themes of mission, doctrine and social responsibility refer to so many of the central concerns of the churches, but these remained three separate movements until the second half of the twentieth century.

When one considers the scope of these new perspectives, it is clear that the churches' horizons were opening up in many different directions at the turn of the century. It was a time of extremely creative and ambitious thinking, a reaching out for the possibilities of a new century. With the impetus given by missionary concern, the churches were now assessing their total lives and looking for new and better ways of relating to one another and to the world in which they were placed or, rather, into which they were sent with a great mission, the communication of the gospel and the engagement of the church with the life of the world.

From the Continuation Committee to the International Missionary Council

While Edinburgh 1910 undoubtedly was a thoroughly prepared and ultimately most historic conference, its emphasis lay in the concept of the Christian world organising for the conversion of the non-Christian world and thereby advancing civilisation itself. There was thus a curious linking of sacred and secular goals that betrayed what can only be described as a certain Western arrogance. Andrew Walls writes: 'In 1910, the Edinburgh World Missionary Conference was too concerned with the impact of Western education and "civilisation" upon the non-Western world to take much account of the independent cultural heritage of the newer churches.'[1] Brian Stanley has similarly noted how Edinburgh 1910 divided the world into Christian and non-Christian sectors, geographically, and as a conference was dominated by the juxtaposition of East and West. He goes on to point out: 'The other implication of the east-west language that shaped the mentality of Edinburgh 1910 was its covert relegation of the south – Latin America, Oceania and Africa – to a decidedly secondary place in the missionary agenda, well behind the Asian orient where it was believed that the most decisive battles of missionary confrontation with other religions and ideologies would be fought.'[2] It is surely strikingly ironic, with the benefit of hindsight, to see how explosive the growth of Christianity in Africa has in fact turned out to be, compared to the East. Somewhere in that course of events lies a very important reminder for the churches of how plans for church growth should recognise, more clearly and more faithfully, the capacity of the Spirit to move unexpectedly and to confound human predictions, no matter how wise or important their source may be.

The Edinburgh 1910 continuation committee was formed towards the end of the conference and its membership of thirty-five was overwhelmingly Western, with only five members from outside Britain, America and continental Europe. Keith Clements, noting that those five were from South Africa, Australasia, Japan, China and India, points out that it was the continuation committee precisely of the Edinburgh conference, which itself had been made up of representatives of the missionary organisations which, in turn, were largely led by white, Western men. Nonetheless, Clements goes on to comment that 'within its obvi-

1. A. F. Walls, *The Missionary Movement in Christian History: Studies in the Transmission of Faith*, New York: Orbis, and Edinburgh: T. & T. Clark, 2007, p 180
2. B. Stanley, *The World Missionary Conference, Edinburgh 1910*, op. cit., p 306

ous limitations, the membership of the Continuation Committee did signify a real advance in interchurch relationships', and asks rhetorically how many other bodies, at a time of often bitter Anglican-Nonconformist rivalry, could have brought such figures willingly together.[3] Considering the nature of the then existing church relationships, one can indeed see the progress of Edinburgh 1910 itself, in this regard, consolidated in the continuation committee.

At its meeting in 1911, the continuation committee decided to launch the journal, the *International Review of Missions*, which would be edited by J. H. Oldham who had been the general secretary of Edinburgh 1910; this was a singularly important decision, marking what Clements has described as 'another definitive stage in the ecumenical movement' since it was the first international and ecumenical journal.[4] However, as far as the continuation committee itself was concerned, a fundamental structural problem was undeniable: it was not directly representative of the missionary organisations but, rather, of the Edinburgh conference. A more effective way of bringing the actual organisations together, in a truly mutually committed joint body, was needed.

Eventually, in 1921, this need was met with the decision to form what would be the International Missionary Council, but the dreadful experience of the First World War was first to have a dramatic impact on missionary thinking. Not only did it completely disrupt travel and communication, but the trauma of World War I led the churches to reflect on such a very fundamental theme as human nature itself, which was increasingly seen as unsure because of its now self-evident capacity for inhuman acts on such a massive scale. There now had to be some serious theological 'stock taking' in the light of what had been a most cruel conflict which had inflicted truly devastating damage on humanity's self-confidence. Alasdair Heron has written of World War I that it 'did not only transform the political and military map: by the destruction which it wrought, unparalleled in previous

3. K. Clements, *Faith on the Frontier: A Life of J.H. Oldham*, Edinburgh: T. & T. Clark and Geneva: WCC, 1999, pp 101f
4. Ibid., p 107

human history in its scale, it hurled a black question mark against the confidence in the onward and upward progress of Christian civilisation which had so strongly characterised liberal theology, and forced the bitter question whether the advanced theological thought of the nineteenth century as a whole had not been far too unaware of the darker side of human nature, too optimistic about innate human capacity for good'.[5]

C. G. Brown, in his *Religion and Society in Twentieth-Century Britain*, records how 22 percent of British men fought during World War I (5.7 million), of whom 705,000 were killed. Quite apart from this massive loss of life there was, of course, injury on an enormous scale, as well as a consequent questioning of just how the nation was led into such a tragedy; the governing class – and it was a class – was deeply resented. It is hardly surprising that the experience of the First World War had a spiritually devastating effect.

Brown also records the mounting evidence between 1918 and 1919 that the working class, especially male soldiers, were turning away from the churches. He writes: 'The Great War presents the social historian of religion with some contradiction. On the one side, as many traditional church historians have suggested, the First World War seemed a watershed because trench warfare was a shock to men's faith, and because the strategies and systems at the disposal of the churches to sustain popular religious activism – notably confrontational evangelism – were gravely discredited in the context of rising social-class antagonisms. Other historians have located the war's impact in the context of long-term secularisation, drawing on the view of contemporary churchmen that British working-class men were in haemorrhage from organised Christianity in a combined rejection of deference to social elites and God.' Brown goes on to observe that much of what at the time was understood as loss of faith was actually loss of Edwardian reverence for social authority, adding somewhat

---

5. A.I.C. Heron, *A Century of Protestant Theology*, Guildford and London: Lutterworth Press, 1980, p. 69

reassuringly that while the class system was changing, popular Christian faith remained resilient.[6]

Another historian, Roger Lloyd, provides further analysis of the trend when he indicates how those who survived World War I were drained and weary, disillusioned and resentful. Lloyd movingly describes the developing scene: 'No historian will ever be able to write happily about English history between 1919 and 1939, and it would be hard to find any other period of twenty years in which more people were unhappy, or more people who also believed that their unhappiness was neither necessary, nor of their own making, but due to some betrayal of the powers-that-be, the custodians and vested interests of the old order, or to the indifference of God himself.'[7] Alan Wilkinson also refers to the widespread sense of disillusionment with established leaders in politics, the church and the forces during and after World War I.[8]

The First World War made for difficulties in international relationships in Edinburgh 1910's continuation committee. German missions were a very significant part of the global missionary endeavour but, as Keith Clements has written, most of the German missionary work was in British territories or territories soon to be seized by the British. He adds: 'Overnight, therefore, many of the German missionaries became aliens on enemy territory, and subject to British governmental measures dictated by the exigencies of war. Many were interned or repatriated. The fate of their missions became the single most contentious issue between the Germans and the "remnant symbol" of the Continuation Committee ...' Clements records, however, how J. H. Oldham was undoubtedly influential when it came to Article 438 of the 1919 Versailles peace treaty, exempting German missions from Allied appropriation of property towards the payment of war debts.[9]

Towards the end of the war, an emergency committee of co-

6. C. G. Brown, *Religion and Society in Twentieth-Century Britain*, Harlow, UK: Pearson Education Limited, 2006, pp 92, 107 and 111

7. R. Lloyd, *The Church of England 1900-1965*, London: SCM, 1966, pp 241 and 243

8. A. Wilkinson, *The Church of England and the First World War*, London: SCM, 1978, p 291

9. op. cit., pp 147 and 164 respectively

operating missions was created – the continuation committee not functioning normally – and then, in 1920 and with German partic- ipation, a rather *ad hoc* international missionary meeting was held at Chateau Crans in Switzerland. Attendance at Crans included both the continuation and emergency committees and the main objective of those who gathered at the chateau undoubtedly was the establishment of a new global missionary structure. This ob- jective was met with the creation of the International Missionary Committee; only the details remained to be worked out. Clements records the historic importance of how at a meeting in the follow- ing year at Lake Mohonk in New York 'eleven years after Edinburgh, the structure and aims of a permanent body were at last agreed', with its name finally determined as the 'International Missionary Council' (IMC). Thus took shape the formal expres- sion of international missionary endeavour that was envisaged at Edinburgh 1910 and that would be pivotal for the Protestant churches' missionary work in the coming decades.

The 1928 Jerusalem conference of the IMC was the first major international missionary conference since Edinburgh 1910, focus- ing largely on Christianity's relationship with other religions, the relationship between the younger and older churches, and the challenge of advancing secularism. The Jerusalem meeting – un- fortunately held without German participation due to post-war circumstances and certain concerns about aspects of the agenda – saw much greater participation of the younger churches than had been the case at Edinburgh, not least as a result of their growth and the ability of their leaders. There had been a real resentment among the younger churches of western dominance in the mis- sionary endeavour and their much greater participation in the Jerusalem meeting certainly did much to correct that imbalance.

Its final message, the Jerusalem conference recognised that 'just because in Jesus Christ the light that lighteneth every man shone forth in its full splendour, we find rays of that same light where he is unknown or even is rejected'. Nonetheless, the mes- sage also called on those adhering to non-Christian religions 'to join with us in the study of Jesus Christ'.[10]

---

10. *The Christian Message - Jerusalem Meeting Report, Vol 1*, Oxford University Press, 1928, pp. 490f

Faith and Order

The US Episcopal Bishop of Western New York, the Rt Rev. Charles Brent, brought home from Edinburgh 1910 a real vision of church unity. He was convinced that the Edinburgh experience had encouraged the belief that a similar world conference on faith and order matters could well be equally productive. This in itself was testimony to the success of the Edinburgh world missionary conference: it had created hopes and inspired efforts on a wider ecumenical and truly ambitious scale, even though faith and order matters had been excluded from its agenda. So, in October of 1910 precisely the proposal of a world conference on faith and order was brought to and endorsed by the General Convention of the US Episcopal Church, meeting in Cincinnati. The motion read: 'That a Joint Commission be appointed to bring about a Conference for the consideration of questions touching Faith and Order, and that all Christian Communions throughout the world which confess Our Lord Jesus Christ as God and Saviour be asked to unite with us in arranging for and conducting such a Conference.'

A committee was appointed by the US Episcopal convention to take further the vision of a world conference on the subject, comprising representatives of all Christian bodies throughout the world. A deputation travelled to Britain and Ireland in 1912 and secured support for the initiative; other Protestant churches in the United States had also signalled their support. The First World War brought the initiative to a halt; indeed, the trauma not only ended all international travel for the purpose of consultation and planning, but also created its own difficulties in terms of relations between the churches. However, the initiative was kept alive in America during the war; an American preparatory conference was held in 1916 and the initiative was resumed on an international scale immediately after the war. In 1919 a deputation travelled to Europe and the East. Co-operation in the venture was readily forthcoming from the churches, including the Orthodox, but not from the Vatican nor, in fact, immediately from some continental Protestant churches.

Tissington Tatlow has described the rather exotic nature of the American deputation's journey to meet the Orthodox leaders:

'The deputation planned first of all to visit Greece, but it took much longer to get there than they expected, owing to delays consequent upon the war. A French cruiser and military motor-cars, an American submarine and private cars took them on a zig-zag route to Athens, where they spent nine days. They were given every opportunity of presenting the plan of the World Conference, including a visit to the Holy Synod.'[11]

Following discussions with Orthodox leaders in Athens, the delegation was assured of their approval of the plan for a world conference on faith and order. The US Episcopal Church was congratulated on having undertaken such a 'noble effort'.

Similar success was met with other Orthodox churches, though the delegation was unable to visit Russia, or indeed Germany, because of prevailing circumstances in those countries. It transpired, however, that there was some unease within the German Protestant church, and among other continental Protestant churches, about the proposed world conference as it was widely seen as advancing an essentially Anglican agenda.

While the delegation's reception at the Vatican was cordial, the following was the official response: 'The Holy Father, after having thanked them for their visit, stated that as successor of St Peter and Vicar of Christ he had no greater desire than that there should be one fold and one shepherd. His Holiness added that the teaching and practice of the Roman Catholic Church regarding the unity of the visible church of Christ was well known to everybody and therefore it would not be possible for the Catholic Church to take part in such a Congress as the one proposed. His Holiness, however, by no means wished to disapprove of the Congress in question for those who are not in union with the Chair of Peter, on the contrary, he earnestly desires and prays that if the Congress is practicable, those who take part in it may by the Grace of God see the light and become reunited to the visible Head of the Church, by whom they will be received with open arms.'[12]

---

11. Tissington Tatlow, *The World Conference on Faith and Order*, in *A History of the Ecumenical Movement 1517-1948*, ed R. Rouse & S.C. Neill, London: SPCK, 1954, p 414
12. Ibid., p 416

The nonetheless generally very successful initiatives for a world conference on faith and order that were taken by the US Episcopal Church, together with the formation of commissions around the world, led to a 1920 meeting of a preparatory conference in Geneva: representatives of some 70 autonomous churches around the world gathered in the Swiss city under the presidency of Bishop Brent himself. The Geneva conference appointed a continuation committee, which itself divided into two sub-committees, one dealing with business and the other with the actual agenda ('subjects'). Moreover, at the 1920 Geneva meeting, progress was made towards the inclusion of those hesitating Protestant churches in the endeavour towards a world conference.

The continuation committee, meeting immediately after the Geneva preparatory gathering, drew up certain doctrinal questions for consideration by the churches, focusing on the extent to which agreement in faith matters would be required in a reunited church and on the question of creedal statements. The continuation committee met for a second time in 1925 in Stockholm, when it was decided to hold the world conference two years later, with an agenda addressing the issue of unity itself, the nature and mission of the church, the common confession of faith, and ministry and sacraments.

The First World Conference on Faith and Order opened at the University of Lausanne on 3 August, 1927, with 394 representatives of a wide spectrum of 108 churches present (Lutheran, Reformed, Old Catholic, Orthodox, Anglican, Methodist, Congregationalist, Baptist and Disciples of Christ). In his sermon at the opening service, Bishop Charles Brent captured the historic nature of the gathering as well as articulating what undoubtedly was a sacred challenge: 'The call to unity is like the flow of a river; it never ceases. It has been sounding with varying accent through the successive generations since the beginning. To us it has of late come with new force through the voice of God's Spirit speaking to the many divided communions of our day, as the call of a shepherd to his scattered flock. We have responded to his call. We are gathered here at his bidding. He presides over us. In proportion to our obedience to his guidance we shall be able to promote his will

and embrace it as our own. He appeals to us to hush our prejudices, to sit lightly to our opinions, to look on the things of others
as though they were our very own – all this without slighting the
convictions of our hearts or our loyalty to God. It can be done. It
must be done.'[13]

After its serious deliberations on the various themes, the conference issued reports to be circulated among the churches. On the
call to unity, the representatives clearly had been only too aware
of the lessons learned at the Edinburgh 1910 world missionary
conference, with the churches in the mission field known already
to be making such forward strides towards unity that profoundly
challenged the churches represented at Lausanne. The gospel itself was portrayed as a joyful message of hope for the world and
the church was described as possessing certain fundamental characteristics – holy scripture, the profession of faith in God as incarn-
ate and revealed in Christ, the acceptance of Christ's commission
to preach the gospel to every creature, the observance of the sacraments, a ministry of preaching and administration of the sacraments,
and being a spiritual fellowship. However, differences remained
amongst the representatives as to the extent to which the church,
as thus described, found expression in the different denominations. There was much agreement on the common confession of
faith, although certain difficulties were identified regarding the
creeds, in particular the *filioque* clause and the differing perspectives of the Orthodox and the western churches.[14] Differences were
also highlighted regarding ministry and sacraments, but the
Lausanne meeting nonetheless saw itself as essentially a starting
point for the churches in what would be an ongoing faith and
order movement. Indeed, so it was to be.

The approach of the world conference had been very much a
comparative one, but the context made that necessary. This was,
after all, the first such gathering. Despite Bishop Brent's initial

---

13. *Faith and Order – Proceedings of the World Conference Lausanne, August
3-21, 1927*, ed H. N. Bate, London: SCM, 1927, p 4
14. The *filioque* clause refers to the Western Church's addition of 'and the
Son' to the Nicene Creed, thereby indicating that the Holy Spirit proceeds from the Father and the Son.

plea to sit lightly by one's own perspectives, a radical outcome from this meeting simply was not to be expected. Anglo-Catholics present objected to the emphasis on ecumenical collaboration, as opposed to unity in faith and order, in the report of the Lausanne conference's section dealing with 'The Unity of Christendom and the relation thereto of existing Churches'.

This had been a very difficult section, as was indicated by one of its chairmen, the Church of Ireland Archbishop of Armagh, Dr D'Arcy, who referred to the almost insuperable difficulties the members of the section had faced.[15] It was eventually agreed to accept the report but to request the continuation committee to consider the matter further. The report stated: 'In preparation for closer fellowship, each section of the church should seek more intimate knowledge of faith and life, worship and order in other communions. Differences founded in complicated historic developments may sometimes prove to be less important than they are supposed to be. As our several communions come to understand each other better they will refrain from competitive propaganda to exalt the one by depreciating the other.'[16] Yet the experience in the missionary context, so clearly recalled in the Lausanne conference's final report for the churches, provided a real impetus: if the young, indigenous churches had a driving vision of unity, no less was appropriate in the historic denominations.

Life and Work
If the Protestant churches in Germany in particular had their initial reservations about the US Episcopal Church's faith and order initiative, there were no similar hesitations when it came to 'life and work'.

The nineteenth century sense of social responsibility in the churches was expressed in varying ways, typically in the home missions. However, following the First World War, it became clear to many in the churches that the vast social needs that existed could not be met through voluntary or charitable effort alone, but that the political dimension had to be more fundamentally recognised. The growing distance between working people and the

15. Ibid., p 435
16. Ibid., p 436

churches, at least in Britain, left the latter more than ever concerned to identify directly with working people's needs. This gave important impetus to the social gospel theology, such as lay behind the international life and work movement.

J. H. Oldham, who had been general secretary of Edinburgh 1910 and a founder of the International Missionary Council as well as its secretary and editor of the *International Review of Missions*, was a most influential figure in church life, and his thinking developed in the post-war context so that his view of mission became, as Keith Clements has described it, characteristically more 'holistic'. Clements has stressed the importance of this for the developing ecumenical movement and the eventual World Council of Churches: 'There is a somewhat mythicised retrospective view which assumes that, over against the socio-political concerns brought into the WCC through 'Life and Work', the IMC was always the standard-bearer of "mission as evangelism". Whatever later developments may have been, such a polarisation was anathema to Oldham. For him, the IMC agenda from the start had to include what we today call "justice and peace" issues.'[17]

One of the major concerns of Oldham, as highlighted by Clements, was that of race. In fact, Oldham's *Christianity and the Race Problem* (1924) was a seminal work and revealed a prophetic voice in its author, not least when he wrote that whenever racial segregation is imposed 'a vital and essential truth of Christianity is compromised'.[18] For Oldham, Christian mission could not simply be defined geographically, as had been the prevailing mind-set at Edinburgh 1910, but had to go much deeper. In short, Oldham's concerns had shifted very clearly in the direction of life and work.

A series of conferences in England held under the auspices of the Interdenominational Social Service Council, founded in 1911, led to the 1924 Conference on Christian Politics, Economics and Citizenship ('Copec') and on the continent similar Christian

17. K. Clements, *Changing Concepts of World Mission, 1910-1948: The Role of J. H. Oldham,* Univ. Cambridge 'Currents in World Christianity' Position Paper 101, p 5
18. J. H. Oldham, *Christianity and the Race Problem*, London: SCM, 1924, pp 282f, as in Clements, ibid., p 6

social movements were also advanced. However, already before World War I, the churches were heavily involved in promoting Christian principles in the arena of international affairs, in particular the promotion of world peace, but the terrible experience of 1914-1918 led to an intensification of efforts in the churches towards peace, reconciliation and social responsibility, a development that was epitomised in the approach of J. H. Oldham. Parallel trends were taking place within the Roman Catholic Church and there was some contact across the ecumenical divide. However, in Protestant circles, the life and work movement had been born, and its first international conference – the Universal Conference on Life and Work – was held in Stockholm in 1925.

The Archbishop of Uppsala, Nathan Söderblom, had tried in 1914 to galvanise church leaders internationally in witnessing for peace. As an archbishop in a neutral country, he had felt all the more keenly that this was his role. The statement that he asked the church leaders to sign was entitled, 'For peace and Christian Fellowship': 'The war is causing untold distress. Christ's body, the church, suffers and mourns. Mankind in its need cries out, O Lord, how long? ... We, the servants of the church, address to all those who have power or influence in the matter an earnest appeal seriously to keep before their eyes, in order that bloodshed soon may cease ... Our faith perceives what the eye cannot always see: the strife of nations must finally serve the dispensation of the Almighty, and all the faithful in Christ are one. Let us therefore call upon God that he may destroy hate and enmity, and in mercy ordain peace for us. His will be done!'[19]

While this statement was straightforward and apparently uncontroversial, it did not gain that many signatures,[20] not least be-

---

19. As in S. Nell, *Men of Unity*, London: SCM, 1960, pp 27f

20. It was signed by representatives of the Federal Council of Churches of Christ in America, the Primates of Sweden, Norway and Denmark, as well as by leading church figures and organisations in Holland and Switzerland and by the Archbishop of Abo (Finland) and Bishop Farancz in Siebenburgen, the latter two of belligerent states. (cf. ed G. K. A. Bell, *The Stockholm Conference 1925 – The Official report of the Universal Christian Conference on Life and Work held in Stockholm, 19-30 August 1925*, OUP and London: Humphrey Milford, 1926, p 3)

cause it was difficult for church leaders at the time in those nations involved in the conflict to be detached from, or impartial about, the sense of outrage at injustice and aggression. Different sides in conflicts do see things differently, each confident in its own position. Yet, in the aftermath a more objective assessment of events becomes possible through rigorous historical analysis and the acceptance of stark realities. While there were international church efforts for peace, it was inevitably a difficult and challenging witness.

In the post-war situation, the enthusiastic Söderblom remained undeterred in his efforts to bring the churches together, internationally, to confer on the great issues of the day and to apply to them the fundamental principles of the gospel. Yet, however pivotal Söderblom's role was in gathering the 1925 Stockholm conference together, the life and work movement was in fact the fruit of much earlier thinking on Christian social responsibility and, in a way, gave that thinking new direction.

The Social Gospel

Already in the nineteenth century, the application of Christian theology to the practicalities of workers' conditions became a 'live' issue. The Anglican divine, F. D. Maurice (1805-1872) was a leading thinker on Christianity and social reform and was one of the foremost of the Christian Socialists, an English movement prompted in particular by the hardship of the 'Hungry Forties' – the potato famine that was most severely experienced in Ireland, but also affected much of northern Europe. The principles of this liberal theology crossed the Atlantic and gave rise to the social gospel movement, championing the rights of working people and questioning capitalist individualism. While social gospel thinking was largely based on the concepts of progress towards the kingdom and a high view of human nature, both of which suffered greatly as a result of the First World War, the approach proved resilient at least in so far as witness for social justice became a permanent dimension of thinking about gospel and mission.

Perhaps the leading exponent of social gospel thinking in the United States was Walter Rauschenbusch (1861-1918). At the age of 25 he became the pastor of the Second German Baptist Church in the 'Hell's Kitchen', or Clinton, district of Manhattan, New York. His personal encounter with the hardships of poverty and deprivation in the city had a dramatic effect on his thinking. He wrote: 'I saw how men toiled all their life long, hard toilsome lives, and at the end had almost nothing to show for it; how strong men begged for work and could not get it in the hard times; how little children died – oh, the children's funerals! They gripped my heart ...'[21]

The social gospel came as a challenge, fundamentally, to economic injustice. There had naturally always been in the churches a concern for social welfare and, in the missionary context, that concern is particularly clear when one considers missionaries' involvement in education and medical care. Yet, the social gospel took this concern a step further in asserting that conversion itself applied not only to individuals but also to institutions and nations – society at large. Janet Fishburn has written: 'The issue between liberals and conservatives was not whether the gospel had social implications. Both had believed that it did since the time of 'the Second Awakening' in the 1830s. The test of a genuine conversion was whether the experience issued in good works or not. Around 1880 some pastors responded to new social problems like labour conditions and wages, poverty and the moral life of the poor. It was then that pastors and professors who were aware of the systemic dimensions of social problems began to address these issues in terms of "the social gospel".'[22] It was precisely such a recognition of the systemic aspect of sin that drove the proponents of the social gospel to see the gospel as addressing this dimension of life, and not solely the individual. The message of the gospel is, indeed, a message for the whole world and is narrowed too much when it is understood purely in terms of the individual and when the corporate dimension of salvation – the life of the kingdom – is

---

21. W. Rauschenbusch, *The Kingdom of God*, pp 265, as in H. Beckley, *Passion for Justice*, Louisville, Kentucky: Westminster / John Knox Press, 1992, p 29
22. J. Fishburn, *The Social Gospel as Missionary Ideology*, Univ. Cambridge 'Currents in World Christianity' Position Paper 54, p 18

seen only in terms of 'me'. Rather, the message of the gospel is for each and for all, addressing the need of the world in all its dimensions.

The social gospel movement taught that the addressing of the systemic was fundamental to the gospel which was applicable not only to 'me' but also to institutional life in all its forms and to peoples and nations. Rauschenbusch could conclude, after a comprehensive historical analysis, that the essential purpose of Christianity was 'to transform society into the kingdom of God by regenerating all human relations and reconstituting them in accordance with the will of God.'[23]

This broadening out of gospel implications was, in fact, largely driven by the social injustices of an overly individualistic capitalism. So, Rauschenbusch wrote: 'Our laws and social institutions have so long taught men that their property is their own, and that they can do what they will with their own, that the church has uphill work in teaching that they are not owners, but administrators. Our industrial individualism neutralises the social consciousness created by Christianity.'[24] He goes on, trenchantly, to point out the irony of how those who championed individualism also championed the home, the school and the church – all three being fundamentally social or 'communistic' institutions in their own right.[25] In terms of political philosophy, Rauschenbusch saw an inherent human draw towards the replacement of primitive human communism, with which society could no longer cope, with a higher form of communism which had as yet proved unattainable. However, it was precisely here that the vision of the kingdom was so relevant for, he wrote, 'there cannot really be any doubt that the spirit of Christianity has more affinity for a social system based on solidarity and human fraternity than for one based on selfishness and mutual antagonism.'[26]

---

23. W. Rauschenbusch, *Christianity and the Social Crisis*, Louisville, Kentucky: Westminster/John Knox Press, 1991, ad loc (originally published by The Macmillan Company, 1907)
24. Ibid., p 388
25. Ibid. p 390
26. Ibid., p 397

The concept of the individual before God was not displaced in Rauschenbusch's thinking, however. Janet Fishburn has pointed out how his family background was thoroughly missionary in character, but also how he accused the 'old' and overly individualistic theology of appealing, essentially, to the individual's self-interest and excluded the social dimension. However, Fishburn further comments: 'Although Rauschenbusch never questioned conversion as part of evangelism, he believed his call was to proclaim "the social gospel". Contemporaries who knew him through his books would not have detected his larger loyalty to personal evangelism or missions.'[27] Nonetheless, in a telling instruction towards the start of his book, *A Theology for the Social Gospel*, Rauschenbusch told readers to take for granted, in all that followed, 'the familiar experiences and truths of personal evangelism'.[28]

Before considering the first life and work conference at Stockholm in 1925, and particularly in light of the ecumenical interest of the present study, it is appropriate to take note of another social justice voice that was almost contemporaneous with Rauschenbusch, but Roman Catholic – that of the American cleric and theologian, John Ryan (1869-1945).

In his very scholarly comparative analysis of the thinking of Rauschenbusch, Ryan and the later Reinhold Niebuhr, Harlan Beckley notes how Ryan, unlike Rauschenbusch or indeed Niebuhr, did not need to be converted to social justice concern. Rather, Ryan came from Irish immigrant farming stock, in the American mid-west, his outlook shaped not only by the Irish immigrant community's memories of deprivation in Ireland but also, and no doubt more critically, by post-American Civil War economic policies that, as Beckley notes, produced deflation, declining farm prices and high interest rates.[29] This economic concern combined with Catholic moral theology to produce in Ryan a

---

27. J. Fischburn, op. cit., p 21
28. W. Rauschenbusch, *A Theology for the Social Gospel*, Nashville: Abingdon, 1917, 1945, p 9, as in J. Fishburn, op. cit., p 21
29. H. Beckley, *Passion for Justice: Retrieving the Legacies of Walter Rauschenbusch, John A. Ryan and Reinhold Niebuhr*, Louisville, Kentucky: Westminster/John Knox Press, 1992, p 111

formidable Catholic force which, if not exactly 'social gospel', certainly shared many social gospel characteristics.

In fact, Ryan found considerable impetus for his thinking in Pope Leo XIII's 1891 encyclical, *Rerum Novarum*, which gave legitimacy and approval to the emergent Catholic social movement. While *Rerum Novarum* had affirmed the natural right to private property, it also emphasised the role of the state in protecting workers' rights and defending social justice. It is not surprising that two of Ryans' works were entitled *Distributive Justice* and *A Living Wage: Its Ethical and Economic Aspects*. It is, however, somewhat surprising, at least by modern norms, that Ryan and Rauschenbusch, despite so many common concerns, did not interact or respond to each other's work but pursued their interests with mutual detachment. Such was, of course, reflective of the then current state of Protestant-Roman Catholic relations. However, there can be no doubt that clear parallels are to be found between the social gospel, the Christian socialist movement in England and the Catholic social movement. All responded to the abuses of unbridled capitalism which were so ferociously experienced by working people as a result of industrialisation.

Stockholm 1925

Archbishop Söderblom stood in this liberal and socially concerned theological and moral tradition, with his conviction that the church was called to play its part in the Christian transfiguration of the social order. Rather than being crushed by the 1914-18 experience, the social gospel took on a new urgency and to a large extent was embodied in the life and work movement which made for a unified voice of Protestant and Orthodox churches in relation to the pressing, post-war social witness of the churches.

The aim of the 1925 Stockholm 'Universal Christian Conference on Life and Work', as set out by its planners two years earlier at a meeting in Zurich, was threefold: (1) to unite the churches in 'common practical work', (2) to give the churches a common voice, and (3) 'to insist that the principles of the gospel be applied to the solution of contemporary social and international problems'. Faith and order matters had been explicitly ruled out. Furthermore, the uniqueness of the Stockholm conference, and the life and work movement in general, was clear in so far as the conference differed from the World Alliance for Promoting International Friendship through the Churches in that it dealt with matters that were beyond, and different in emphasis from, issues of peace and good relations between the nations.[30]

While its extensive formal message lamented the fact that not all Christian communions had been represented at the conference (the Roman Catholic Church, in particular, had not been a participant), the text also recognised that the Stockholm meeting had been 'only a beginning'.[31] In clear echoes of social gospel thinking, the message indicated: 'Thus in the sphere of economics we have declared that the soul is the supreme value, that it must not be subordinated to the rights of property or to the mechanism of industry ... Property should be regarded as a stewardship for which an account must be given to God. Co-operation between capital and labour should take the place of conflict, so that employers and employed alike may be enabled to regard their part in industry as the fulfilment of a vocation.'[32]

Speaking in support of the message, which was approved with overwhelming support, Dr von Pechmann (Germany) could declare that while he had come 'with very modest expectations and not without serious fear and anxiety', he found his expectations 'far surpassed' and his fears 'undermined and confounded'.[33]

The beginning of the life and work movement that was signalled at Stockholm in 1925 had indeed been an auspicious occasion, although of course the Stockholm meeting was itself the culmination of the movement in its initial phase. Nevertheless, to bring the movement further, in the mode of Edinburgh 1910, a continuation committee was formed. This was needed because there was so much unfinished work – Stockholm had only been a beginning. While the conference had set clearly before the churches the need for an ecumenical response to the great social and econ-

30. cf ed G. K. A. Bell, *The Stockholm Conference 1925*, op. cit., p 1
31. Ibid., p 711
32. Ibid., p 712
33. Ibid., p 719

omic issues of the day, the difficulties in attaining this in an effect-ive manner had become apparent. It was also clear that the churches needed to reflect more deeply, in a theological way, on human nature itself and social life. As the German Prälat D. Schoell could say: 'There is no single sphere of life in which the Christian standard can be surrendered; but there is perhaps no sphere where a fresh thinking out, simplification and develop-ment of these principles is not necessary.'[34]

The Stockholm conference therefore had succeeded in giving focus to the concerns of life and work and had revealed the need for deeper theological reflection to underpin the ecumenical re-sponse to socio-economic problems. However, just how this life and work movement could relate in practical terms to those prob-lems was bound to be a very big question. The church can give some direction to thinking and attitudes, but what could the church really do in the face of the deep economic recession that characterised the period? While there had been a typical emphasis on wartime heavy industry, the post-World War I situation brought recession, mass unemployment and accompanying social protest. Writing of the inter-war years, Norman Davies has ob-served: 'On the moral front, one has to note the extreme contrast between the material advancement of European civilisation and the terrible regression in political and intellectual values. Militarism, fascism and communism found their adherents not only in the manipulated masses of the most afflicted nations, but [also] amongst Europe's most educated elites and in its most democratic countries.'[35]

It was in such a maelstrom of intellectual, social and political life that the life and work movement sought to articulate a Christian vision. Such a witness was vital if the church was to be true to its Lord and to itself.

---

34. Ibid., p 221
35. N. Davies, *Europe: A History,* OUP, 1996, p 899

CHAPTER FOUR

From the 1930 to the 1960s

The missionary, faith and order and life and work movements, despite the undoubted practical challenges posed by international recession, continued undeterred in the 1930s, holding landmark gatherings in Tambaram (India), Edinburgh and Oxford respectively. The First World War had thrown a major question mark over the dominance of western 'civilisation' and the sense of superiority of the church in Europe and America, engendering increasing confidence within the younger churches established in the mission field – confidence in their faith, church life and cultures. The Second World War did the same, yet again. The decades from the 1930s to the 1960s were to see major developments affecting all three movements.

The Missionary Movement 1938-1963
The International Missionary Council's 1928 meeting in Jerusalem, as we noted in the last chapter, saw much greater participation of the younger churches than had been the case at the 1910 Edinburgh world missionary conference; this trend continued yet further at Tambaram in 1938. At that gathering over 50 per cent of the delegates were from those churches. Moreover, the competence and spiritual maturity of their representatives were striking. This was the first non-Western ecumenical gathering and in itself marked the beginning of a shift of emphasis in thinking and attitude towards a sense of the mission of the church as one mission in which all – the older and younger churches – shared on an equal basis. This shift has been described by Jerald D. Gort as a change of perspective from Western evangelistic outreach to a more holistic concept of mission. Furthermore, as Gort indicates, Tambaram also expressed the view that mission had to do not only with indi-

vidual salvation but also with issues of justice and peace.[1] There were clear resonances with the life and work emphases in that broader concept of mission, but the ecclesiocentric missionary emphasis at Tambaram was soon to give way to the God-centred understanding of mission as epitomised in the *missio Dei* doctrine which affirmed that mission is, first and foremost, God's mission and that the church's place is subsidiary (see further below).

The Tambaram meeting was followed after World War II by an IMC meeting at Whitby, Ontario in 1947. As well as attempting to recover relations following the moral and physical destruction of the war, the Whitby meeting marked a further development of the understanding of mission as being fundamentally shared by the older and younger churches, with 'partnership in obedience' being the dominant theme. Kenneth Scott Latourette observes of Whitby that the meeting was marked by an 'equality and mutuality', a shared partnership between the younger and older churches such as had never been known before, and adds: 'This new partnership in obedience to God's will is part of the tomorrow that Whitby experienced as already here. It was not always so. Western churches, the so-called "sending churches", provided the missionaries, supplied the money, and supervised its expenditure. Unfortunately, too, some missionaries were imbued with an attitude of "the white man's burden". Paternalism and the patriarchal missionary at the head of a small Christian community were the all too common results.'[2]

Whitby saw a shift in thinking away from the earlier and more simplistic view of the world as divided between Christian and non-Christian lands. The missiological situation was seen as more subtle than that and the developing understanding of mission was definitely in a new direction which would become more

---

1. J. D. Gort, *Syncretism and Dialogue: Christian Historical and Earlier Ecumenical Perceptions*, in ed J. D. Gort, H. M. Vroom, R. Fernhout and A. Wessels, *Dialogue and Syncretism: An Interdisciplinary Approach*, Eerdmans, 1989, p. 44
2. K. S. Latourette, *Tomorrow is here: the mission and work of the church as seen from the meeting of the International Missionary Council at Whitby, Ontario, July 5-24, 1947*, Friendship Press, pp 105f

clearly articulated at, and from, the International Missionary Council's 1952 meeting at Willingen in Germany.

There can be no doubt that at and following Edinburgh 1910 there were great hopes for Christian mission in China, no matter how challenging the church there had been as far as *status quo* denominationalism was concerned. Many hopes and much effort had been invested in Chinese mission, but all of that came to an end following 1949 when, after its victory in the Chinese civil war, Mao Zedong's Communist Party of China (CPC) gained control of most of mainland China. The civil war had been running since 1927 as an ideological conflict between the Chinese Nationalist Party, backed by the West, and the CPC, backed by the Soviet Union.

Lesslie Newbigin writes of the great blow to missionary hopes: 'At the World Missionary Conference at Tambaram in 1938, the Chinese delegation had been outstanding in quality. The Chinese church, though small, seemed full of immense promise. Yet, within a few years of the establishment of communist rule in China, missions had been completely eliminated from the country and much of the fruit of their century of work had apparently been destroyed.' But Newbigin goes on to identify a yet deeper wounding in those circumstances in that the communist government in China in fact had been able to accomplish many of the aims of the missions, but which the latter had simply been too weak to bring to reality.[3]

This major blow to the missionary vision created what one might go so far as to characterise as a sense of shock, disorientation and crisis in the mission world. Yet, at the same time and on a more positive note, the parallel faith and order and life and work movements had joined together in the new World Council of Churches, inaugurated in Amsterdam in 1948. The formation of the WCC brought together the older and younger churches across the globe on a fully equal basis and it was precisely this that created another dilemma for the missionary movement: where

---

3. L. Newbigin, *Mission to Six Continents*, in ed H. E. Fey, *The Ecumenical Advance: A History of the Ecumenical Movement, Volume Two, 1948-1968*, London: SPCK, 1970, p 173

exactly did this new context of genuine interdependence leave mission itself? Of course, the West remained a powerful resource, not least when it came to delivering aid, as was done through the WCC, but 'partnership' became the key word. The flow of aid was from churches to churches and not via the traditional missionary conduit. What is more, in turn the younger churches brought vibrancy and challenges of all sorts to the experience of the longer established churches.

It was against such a backdrop that the International Missionary Council's 1952 Willingen (Germany) meeting was held. While initially regarded as not having been particularly visionary – perhaps due to a certain underlying crisis as a result of the context just outlined – with hindsight Willingen is now often celebrated for the theological direction it in fact gave to Protestant missiology, firmly anchoring mission in the trinitarian doctrine of God. This was the *missio Dei* understanding coming to full fruit.

In broadening out the basis for missiological thinking, Willingen enabled a firm linkage between mission and socio-economic issues such as had been represented in the life and work movement, now integrated into the WCC, and also gave impetus to a more positive evaluation of, and approach to, other religions. However, equally, it appears that from Willingen on, mission is less and less seen in traditional evangelistic terms and for that reason Willingen has been described as marking a kind of 'Copernican revolution' in Protestant missiological thought. There is no doubt that there is a fundamental change of perspective here, as the churches not only re-interpret but also seek to re-establish Christian mission in the aftermath of the savage attacks on Western confidence – and mission – brought about by the two World Wars, by the end of mission in now communist China, and by the new state of global church relations brought about in a definitive way by the fellowship of the WCC.

In summarising the findings of Willingen, Karl Hartenstein, who in 1926 had become the director of the Basel Protestant Missionary Society, uses the term *missio Dei*. Hartenstein had been particularly influential in the development of theological thought on religions and what was the *missio Dei* concept of mission. He saw the phenomenon of religion as a universal human attempt to reach out for divine salvation and the *missio Dei* in terms of the church as participating in the much deeper mission that is God's outreach to the world; in that divine outreach the church was an instrument. Mission was an attribute of God and the church served that purpose in the subordinate *missio ecclesiae*. So, mission did not belong to the church but flowed from the heart of God. This emerging more God-centred view of mission provided much scope for the expanding of missionary vision. It affirmed God's action in the secular world, mission not being constricted or confined as a purely ecclesiastical function.

Another advocate of the *missio Dei* concept was H. J. Hoekendijk, an Indonesian-born, Dutch missionary theologian. Hoekendijk was supremely suspicious of 'churchism' and held to a much more dynamic view of God's activity in the world. Bert Hoedemaker has drawn the intriguing parallel of such a view with the traditionally sceptical attitude of evangelicalism with regard to 'church-as-institution', but goes on to characterise Hoekendijk's approach in its distinctive terms: 'The dominant note, however, was the conviction that a preoccupation with church would blind the ecumenical movement to what is really going on in the world – the vast field of humanity in need of *shalom*.'[4]

A growing awareness of how missions had been confused with Western cultural norms, the traumatic experience of war and the questions which both the First and Second World Wars inevitably threw up about Western values and civilisation, and the whole new global geopolitical context all demanded, as Hoedemaker points out, a fundamentally new approach to mission. To a definite extent that had come, certainly, with the recognition of the equal status of younger and older churches such as in Whitby 1947's 'partnership in obedience' theme, but it was the *missio Dei* theology that was to provide a new missionary rationale at an even deeper level. Yet, *missio Dei* thinking also meant leaving behind the overwhelming emphasis on personal, individual evangelistic

---

4. B. Hoedemaker, *The Legacy of J. C. Hoekendijk*, in *The International Bulletin of Missionary Research*, October 1995, p 3

outreach that had been so characteristic of Edinburgh 1910 when 'strategy' had been so fundamental. Where would the strategy lie in the new *missio Dei* world?

While, interestingly, Pentecostals were present at the Willingen meeting, indicating a new dimension to the organised, ecumenical mission 'world', at Willingen there was a fundamental clash between those who saw God's action in the world more or less exclusively as being through the church and those who, like Hoekendijk, shared to varying degrees a certain church-scepticism. However, an American report presented to Willingen, 'Why Mission?', tried to strike what might be seen as some balance in this whole debate in that it argued that the church should take note of the 'signs of the times', of how God was acting in the world and speaking through what was essentially secular life. The *missio Dei* theology stressed God at work in the world but also saw the church as instrument of God's mission – if not the sole instrument.

When the World Council of Churches was formed in 1948, the International Missionary Council was formally 'in association'. Lesslie Newbigin records how one of the sections of the WCC's inaugural assembly in Amsterdam discussed the church's missionary and evangelistic task, and notes how the discussion 'reflected the growing uncertainty within Christendom about the whole matter of evangelism'. In some ways, four years later, Willingen's *missio Dei* concept was a response to a crisis in missiological purpose.

The close link between the International Missionary Council and the new World Council of Churches – and there was an overlap of people who were involved in both organisations – led to the decision at the IMC's next major gathering, in Accra, Ghana in 1958, to integrate with the WCC. While the decision was taken by a large majority, there were some concerns about the potential for the missionary movement's loss of freedom and for a new dependence on church structures to emerge. A sense of some lack of clarity about the way forward for missions also came to the fore. The German Protestant missiologist, Walter Freytag, spoke to the Accra assembly in terms of the loss of direction of missions, pointing to 'mission as God's reality in this world' as the way forward –

very much in the new *missio Dei* mode of thinking. Newbigin records how, reflecting Freytag's thinking, the Accra IMC meeting could declare that 'The Christian world mission is Christ's, not ours' – that is, mission belongs to the church only in a secondary sense.[5]

Yet, if the church was an instrument for God's mission in the world, as the *missio Dei* doctrine taught, it was natural that there should be a closer identification of the ecumenical missionary movement with the new global ecumenical church structure. The decision at Accra to merge with the World Council of Churches led to subsequent deliberation in the member churches of that body and of the International Missionary Council and, at the WCC's 1961 New Delhi assembly, to the formal integration of the IMC. Yet, as Newbigin points out, this integration, highly significant though it undoubtedly was, did not do away with certain questions, not least concerning the purpose of mission, for tension between the evangelistic and the new *missio Dei* approaches persisted and, indeed, has not even yet been finally resolved today.

Quite apart from the formal process of integration of the International Missionary Council, the WCC's 1961 New Delhi assembly considered another matter of important missionary significance, namely, the question of other faiths. The first assembly of the WCC had been in 1948 (Amsterdam), and the second assembly at Evanston, Illinois in 1954. At Evanston there was discussion of Christian relations with other faiths; the assembly's Section II was headed 'The Mission of the Church to those Outside her Life'. A key figure in that debate was D. T. Niles, the Sri Lankan-born missionary and ecumenical leader who had been general secretary of the National Christian Council of Ceylon and also heavily involved in the WCC from its foundation. Niles called for a new approach to evangelism in the light of the renascence of Asian religions. The WCC's central committee later, and accordingly, decided to initiate a study on 'The Word of God and the Living Faiths of Men'; interim findings were reported to the 1961 New Delhi assembly which in turn stressed the place of dialogue as an essential part of Christian witness.

---

5. L. Newbigin, op. cit., pp 184f

The New Delhi assembly's 'Witness' section report placed its emphasis on dialogue in the context of a very balanced approach to the subject of mission. The assembly was, after all, attempting to hold together a whole variety of perspectives. The report started out by affirming that the task of Christian witness was to point to Christ as the true light, adding: 'The work of evangelism is necessary in this and in every age in order that the blind eyes may be opened to the splendour of light.' However, it went on to emphasise the importance and urgency of the study project on 'The Word of God and the Living Faiths of Men', commenting: 'In the churches we have but little understanding of the wisdom, love and power which God has given to men of other faiths and of no faith, or of the changes wrought in other faiths by their long encounter with Christianity. We must take up the conversations about Christ with them, knowing that Christ addresses them through us and us through them.' The report therefore rejoiced in the 'experiments' that were being made in dialogue and in the 'encouragement which they give to those who see the urgent need for new approaches to the task of evangelism in the twentieth century'.[6]

Interfaith dialogue had landed, and two years later, at the 1963 meeting of the WCC's Division on World Mission and Evangelism in Mexico City, dialogue was further affirmed as fundamental to mission. The pattern of Christian mission, it was reported, had to be one of 'constant encounter with the real needs of our age'. The report continued: 'Its form must be that of dialogue, using contemporary language and modes of thought, learning from the scientific and sociological categories, and meeting people in their own situations.' However, despite this clear emphasis, Lesslie Newbigin records that while the Mexico City meeting had conceived of the missionary task 'in the context of what God is doing in the secular events of our time', division still remained over this whole issue, partly due to both a persisting sense of 'crisis of faith' in the Western churches and an as yet incomplete awareness of relevant developing insights.[7]

Despite such continuing debates, the general movement, cer-

6. *New Delhi Speaks*, London: SCM, 1962, ad loc.
7. L. Newbigin, *Mission to Six Continents*, op cit., p 194

tainly among the Protestant church and ecumenical establishment, was from *missio ecclesiae* to *missio Dei*. J. D. Gort has pointed out that this clearly 'played a prime role in the emergence of the newer Christian attitude to people of other faiths and their cultural traditions'.[8] This shift can be observed, very distinctly, in the deliberations of the ecumenical and missionary meetings surveyed here; the *missio Dei* doctrine provided a theological basis for what ultimately was to be the emphasis on interfaith dialogue. While the inherent value of other faiths was certainly affirmed even at Edinburgh 1910, the more open approach of Christians to adherents of other religions was becoming firmly established and the *missio Dei* doctrine provided a fundamental rationale.

While the concerns addressed in this brief survey relate to developments in the Protestant missionary world, it is significant to note that in the year following the Mexico City meeting, 1964, the Roman Catholic theologian, Raymond Panikkar, who had himself been engaged in Christian-Hindu dialogue in India, could write that the Christian attitude to mission in the world 'is not one of bringing God in, but bringing him forth, of discovering Christ'.[9] Such was a classic exposition of the *missio Dei* approach.

The 1930s to the 1960s clearly saw a very significant, changing emphasis in the churches' understanding of mission, a broadening of their approach. This development took place in the context of a questioning of the legitimacy of Western dominance, not least because of the West's own catastrophic failings in the first half of the twentieth century, and the developing experience of real ecclesial interdependence. Questions remained, however, regarding the effectiveness of the more liberal *missio Dei* approach. Was it too intellectually focused? How many people would it actually help bring to a living Christian faith? The 1930s to the 1960s were also decades that saw the other two associated movements, faith and order and life and work, progress in their own ways.

---

8. J. D. Gort, *Syncretism and Dialogue*, op. cit., p 47
9. R. Panikkar, *The Unknown Christ of Hinduism*, London: DLT, 1964, p 45, as in J. D. Gort, *Syncretism and Dialogue*, op. cit., p 47

Faith and Order, Life and Work
and the establishment of the World Council of Churches
The first world faith and order conference had been held in
Lausanne in 1927 (see chap 3). That encounter had been an
important step for the churches in terms of reaching out to one another on the fundamentals of their teaching. In itself it had been a
recognition that the churches in fact needed to do this. In the fast
changing and ever more challenging world in which they sought
to live out their faith and to witness to the gospel, they could no
longer do so in splendid isolation. As the Lausanne meeting had
come to realise in a very fundamental way, if the churches were to
grow together into a deeper fellowship there had to be both a mutual respect and a real understanding of what they each stood for
in terms of the faith itself. Inevitably, however, the Lausanne
meeting could only be a beginning, and it was followed by a second world conference on faith and order in Edinburgh in 1937.

A certain progression is to be discerned in successive world
faith and order conferences from the 1920s to the 1960s. Initially,
the approach was comparative, and that was very understandable
in the circumstances. In the development of relationships there
has to be, first of all, an opportunity of 'getting to know' the other
party. That was also the case for the churches which had for so
long lived more or less unto themselves. The approach of the
churches to one another was at first characteristically tentative
and defensive, but in the process of meeting and debating and
through the consideration of reports in the periods between meetings, the churches began to open up to one another, slowly but
surely.

The Lausanne 1927 meeting set the scene and that approach
continued at Edinburgh 1937. As Lukas Vischer points out, however, after World War II, the faith and order dialogue deepened
and moved beyond comparison – that could not go on for ever,
after all – to a sense of being engaged in a committed process with
the purpose of arriving at a deeper communion between the
churches. Lausanne 1927 had considered the 'marks' of the
church and had expressed commitment to the manifestation of
the unity of the church to the world, and Edinburgh 1937 had con-

sidered the three particular conceptions of unity – co-operation, intercommunion and corporate union. The faith and order move-ment thus was gradually taking on a more definite purpose. At the establishment of the World Council of Churches in 1948, of which the faith and order movement became a commission, there was a sense of needing to go behind the differences to find real common ground on which to build deeper communion.[10]

This was indeed a very significant development and, in itself, posed considerable challenges to the churches that were involved in the exercise. Did they really want to discuss closer unity? What, in any case, did such unity mean? What were the implications for denominational life? These were unsettling questions, no doubt, but they signalled what lay at the very heart of the faith and order movement. What is more, if the churches were going to co-oper-ate more closely, not least in terms of mission, there really did need to be a deeper understanding of what they were actually doing and how they related to one another in that task.

The question of precisely what kind of unity the churches sought was thus an ongoing discussion through the 1930s-1950s, but it came to at least an initial conclusion at the 1961 WCC New Delhi assembly, which reported: 'We believe that the unity which is both God's will and his gift to his church is being made visible as all in each place who are baptised into Jesus Christ and confess him as Lord and Saviour are brought by the Holy Spirit into one fully committed fellowship, holding the one apostolic faith, preaching the one gospel, breaking the one bread, joining in com-mon prayer, and having a corporate life reaching out in witness and service to all, and who at the same time are united with the whole Christian fellowship in all places and all ages in such wise that ministry and members are accepted by all, and that all can act and speak together as occasion requires for the tasks to which God calls his people.'[11]

The 1950 'Toronto Statement' of the WCC's central committee had, very early in the life of the council, declared its own self-un-

---

10. cf L. Vischer, *A Documentary History of the Faith and Order Movement 1927-1963*, Missouri: Bethany Press, 1963, p 13
11. *New Delhi Speaks*, London: SC, 1962, p 55

derstanding as a council of churches, but the New Delhi assembly took ecclesiological thinking further by reflecting on the unity of the church itself, as opposed to defining the kind of unity that exists in a council of churches. There can be no doubt that the New Delhi 'All in each place' statement marked, in its scope and sense of mutual awareness among the churches, a remarkable declaration of intent for the churches and for the ecumenical movement. Certainly, the New Delhi statement left many questions unanswered, questions with which the churches today still are grappling, but it nonetheless set the course and provided a vision for the future. Moreover, the statement made a very clear and direct link between the church's unity and its missionary task: 'In the fulfilment of our missionary obedience the call to unity is seen to be imperative, the vision of one church proclaiming one gospel to the whole world becomes more vivid and the experience and expression of our given unity more real. There is an inescapable relation between the fulfilment of the church's missionary obligation and the recovery of her visible unity.'

The vision of New Delhi here is of the church reaching out to the world in a real corporate life. It was, of course, as we have already indicated, at New Delhi that the International Missionary Council (with its very direct lineage from Edinburgh 1910) was integrated into the life of the World Council of Churches and so, in a very clear way, that assembly links together two very clear visions – the vision of ecclesial unity and the vision of the church acting as one in the fulfilment of its missionary call.

Edinburgh 1937
The faith and order conference that was held in Edinburgh in 1937 and which, like Lausanne ten years earlier, had Protestant and Orthodox but no Roman Catholic representation, had one main benefit over the first conference in Lausanne: the Lausanne continuation committee had planned and prepared for Edinburgh in a very thorough manner. This preparation, together with the fact that there was a substantial continuity of representatives from the Lausanne meeting, gave Edinburgh a great advantage from the start. This was reflected in the depth of the report and the consid-

erable advance in mutual understanding that was achieved. A distinct drawback, however, was the absence of German representation, the German government having ominously refused passports for representatives.

The conference divided into five sections dealing with grace, church and word, the communion of saints, church and ministry and sacraments, and unity. Naturally, as subsequent experience has shown, the issue of ministry and sacraments was a difficult challenge, but nonetheless it was felt that a significant *rapprochement* was reached, beyond what might have been expected, the conference going so far as to consider the form which the ordained ministry might take in 'the united church of the future'. It envisaged an episcopate that was 'both constitutional and representative of the whole church'.[12] Of course, the findings of the conference were not binding on the churches, but were to be offered to the churches for their further reflection. Moreover, some members of the conference were recorded as not believing that a uniform church polity was necessary.

The subject of unity, in fact, raised the most controversy at Edinburgh because it included the proposal for the establishment of a World Council of Churches. The faith and order continuation committee, in the previous year, had received a communication from the life and work movement proposing that a special meeting of both movements and of other ecumenical associations should be held to consider 'the whole ecumenical movement and lay the results before the two conferences at Oxford [life and work, also 1937, see below] and Edinburgh'.[13] Tissington Tatlow records that this debate was marked by 'friction' and that agreement to the proposal to approve a World Council of Churches was reached at Edinburgh only after 'a long and at times heated debate'.[14] A chief opponent was, in fact, the Anglican Bishop of Gloucester, Arthur Headlam, and the conference agreed to a

---

12. Ed L. Hodgson, *The Second World Conference on Faith and Order*, London: SCM, 1938, p 249
13. T. Tatlow, *World Conference on Faith and Order*, in ed R. Rouse and S. Neill, *A History of the Ecumenical Movement, 1517-1948*, op. cit., p 435
14. Ibid., p 433

caveat that, if the churches approved the WCC's formation, the new body 'should be so designed as to conserve the distinctive character and value of each of the movements represented in the two Conferences'.[15] One of Headlam's concerns was that a new council could pass resolutions on public affairs that could cause difficulties for the churches.[16] In fact, W. A. Visser 't Hooft has recorded an undoubtedly disturbing basis for Bishop Headlam's reservations: 'The Bishop of Gloucester's antipathy towards the Life and Work movement was well-known, for he had made no secret of the fact that he disapproved of the position that movement, and in particular its spokesman, the Bishop of Chichester, had taken with regard to the church conflict in Germany. As late as June 1937, Bishop Headlam had stated publicly that National Socialism was not anti-Christian, and that the Third Reich was based upon positive orthodox Christianity.' Visser 't Hooft goes on to point out that in National Socialist circles the life and work movement was considered dangerous, whereas the faith and order movement enjoyed a better reputation.[17] The Edinburgh 1937 report, as well as affirming the distinctiveness of the two movements, expressed reservations regarding the composition of the WCC and the method of appointing its members, but these were seen as details that could be satisfactorily addressed.

Of course, the idea of a World Council of Churches raised many questions of detail, as is the case when any major new structure is being created on the proverbial 'blank piece of paper'. The WCC would be a wholly new ecclesial organisation and questions, for example, as to its basis, *modus operandi*, extent of powers, representative nature, and its authority, were bound to weigh heavily on people's minds. For this reason, one can understand the hesitation of Edinburgh 1937 with regard to the proposal before it, and indeed the 'friction' in the debate, but in the end the

15. Ed L. Hodgson, op. cit., p 269
16. cf W. A. Visser 't Hooft, *The Genesis of the World Council of Churches*, in ed R. Rouse and S. Neill, op. cit., p 703
17. W. A. Visser 't Hooft, *The Genesis and Formation of the World Council of Churches*, Geneva: WCC, 1982, pp 46f

conference saw the bigger picture and endorsed the plan, without committing itself to details.[18]

The Edinburgh 1937 conference concluded an 'Affirmation' which spoke of the representatives' unity founded in Jesus Christ as a unity of 'heart and spirit', but confessing their divisions as contrary to the will of Christ. Nonetheless, the declaration stated very positively: 'We are divided in the outward forms of our life in Christ, because we understand differently his will for his church. We believe, however, that a deeper understanding will lead us towards a united apprehension of the truth as it is in Jesus.' There was also a call for the churches to seek to overcome 'occasions of disunion' and, with a missionary perspective, 'to seek to remove those obstacles to the furtherance of the gospel in the non-Christian world which arise from our divisions'.[19]

Oxford 1937

Just as the 1937 Edinburgh faith and order conference had benefited from the work of a continuation committee following the first faith and order conference ten years earlier, so too with the Oxford 1937 life and work conference, which followed on from the first such meeting in Stockholm in 1925. Equally, the Oxford meeting was held without representatives of the German Protestant Church, its representatives having been refused permission to travel by the German government. For the Oxford conference, as a forum for discussing the church in relation to the state and the economic order, the global social, political and economic circumstances gave urgency and immediate relevance to the discussions that would take place.

First, of course, the 1930s were the years of the great depression, especially in the early years of the decade. The Wall Street crash, the stock market collapse that culminated on 'Black Tuesday', 24 October 1929, symbolises the steep and catastrophic nature of the economic decline that spread across the industrialised nations. The 1920s had been a decade of prosperity – the 'roaring twenties' – but all of a sudden the world changed and op-

---

18. Ibid. p 271
19. Affirmation, ibid., p 275f

timism was replaced with fear. Moreover, the depression was truly international, because global trade suffered, plummeting by up to two-thirds. If World War I had shaken confidence not only in human nature but also in western civilisation, the great depression threw yet another huge question mark over western life. In Germany, American finance for the purpose of post-World War I reconstruction disappeared, leading to soaring unemployment and a concomitant political extremism which saw the end of the Weimar Republic and Hitler coming to power in 1933.

It was against the background of this economic turmoil and rising totalitarianism that the representatives of the mainly Western churches – except the Roman Catholic Church – met at Oxford. They had very fundamental issues to address and they did so with rigour and a remarkable depth of insight. The churches needed to articulate their stance in the context of industrial strife, sheer poverty and rising totalitarianism.

Paul Abrecht notes how in exercising its critique of the current economic order, the Oxford conference stressed how that order challenged the churches in four ways in particular: by its enhancement of acquisitiveness, its inequalities, the irresponsible possession of economic power and the frustration of the sense of Christian vocation.[20] The Swedish church historian and Boston University professor, Nils Ehrenström, notes how J. H. Oldham could describe the essential theme of Oxford 1937 as 'the life and death struggle between Christian faith and the secular and pagan tendencies of our time'. Ehrenström himself declares that the genius of Oxford 1937 was 'that it seized on the central issue of the times, the emergence of the new state which is a parody of the divine society, the church, and yet spoke to the new situation in terms of the unchanging assurances of the faith'.[21]

The Oxford conference placed a great emphasis on the inde-

20. P. Abrecht, *The Development of Ecumenical Social Thought and Action*, in ed H. E. Fey, *The Ecumenical Advance – A History of the Ecumenical Movement, Vol. II, 1948-1968*, p 240

21. N. Ehrenström, *Movements for International Friendship and Life and Work 1925-1948*, in ed R. Rouse and S. Neill, *A History of the Ecumenical Movement 1517-1948*, op. cit., pp 587 and 594

pendence of the church *vis-à-vis* the state, by which the church cannot be used or exploited; the church's freedom must be inviolate. This emphasis on the conference's conviction regarding the independence of the church is found in striking sentences in its report: 'The primary duty of the church to the state is to be the church, namely, to witness for God, to preach his word, to confess the faith before men, to teach both young and old to observe the divine commandments, and to serve the nation and the state by proclaiming the will of God as the supreme standard to which all human wills must be subject and all human conduct must conform. These functions of worship, preaching, teaching, and ministry the church cannot renounce, whether the state consent or not.'[22]

This emphasis contains clear echoes of the thrust of the 1934 Barmen Declaration of the German 'confessing church' which held that the church could not be an organ of the state, a declaration that in effect created two Protestant churches in Germany, the Reichskirche and the Bekennende Kirche ('confessing church'). Nonetheless, the intention of the latter had not been to create a division in the church but, rather, to confess the true faith over against attempts to establish the German Protestant Church's unity 'by means of false doctrine, by the use of force and by insincere practices'. Ehrenström comments that the serious nature of the German government's reaction to the message of the Oxford conference made it clear that the Nazis had discerned the gathering strength of Christian conviction on the issue of church and state.

Of course, while essentially a discussion of social, political and economic issues, the whole tendency of the Oxford conference was towards authentic Christian witness in perplexing and disturbing times. To that extent, certainly, the life and work movement was revealing an essentially missionary dimension, for witness lies at the heart of evangelism. The churches, through the life and work movement, were bearing witness to the eternal truths of the gospel, to fidelity to the Christian way and to the biblical val-

---

22. *The Churches Survey Their Task: The Report of the Conference at Oxford, July 1937, on Church, Community, and State*, London, 1937, p 82

ues of human dignity and freedom. While not formally a 'missionary conference', Oxford 1937 nonetheless was the church engaging in an essentially missionary witness to a lost world.

Both 1937 conferences – Edinburgh on faith and order and Oxford on life and work – marked a significant deepening of each movement and, just as Edinburgh had done, so too Oxford approved the proposal for the merging of the two ecumenical streams in a new World Council of Churches.

Amsterdam 1948

The year 1948 saw the first assembly of the World Council of Churches at Amsterdam, bringing together into a single organisation the faith and order and life and work movements. This did not occur out of the blue, however, but was the culmination of much discussion and consultation that had gathered pace over the years from the end of World War I. Already in 1919, the Ecumenical Patriarchate of Constantinople and Archbishop Söderblom, independently of each other, had begun to formulate proposals for a world body representative of the churches.

The Ecumenical Patriarchate, at its synod in January 1919, took the decision to draw up the terms of an invitation to the other churches to establish a 'League of Churches'. This decision was taken not least in the light of the announcement of plans for a League of Nations, which was ultimately formed following the Treaty of Versailles formally ending the state of war between Germany and the allied nations and signed on 28 June, 1919. A remarkable double feature of the Orthodox initiative was that the proposed League of Churches should embrace all the churches and that its ultimate purpose should be to promote 'the union of all churches in Christian love'.[23] The vision here was therefore ecumenically far-reaching. In 1920, the synod approved a report drawn up by a specially appointed committee and an encyclical was accordingly published in January 1920 – the *Encyclical on the Koinonia of Churches*, addressed 'Unto the Churches of Christ Everywhere'.

23. Statement of Metropolitan Dorotheos of Brussa, *The Ecumenical Review*, Vol XI, 1958-59, p 292

Archbishop Söderblom's proposal for an international ecumenical council was also formulated in 1919, his vision being born of a realisation that the churches of the world needed to be able to speak together to the world, promoting the Christian way more effectively in a truly ecumenical and representative manner. However, while there had been contact between Sweden and Constantinople on the subject, W. A. Visser 't Hooft has recorded that Söderblom himself later spoke of how 'the same thoughts influenced independently the hearts of Christians in different churches and nations'.[24] Indeed, in 1920 J. H. Oldham brought proposals to the international missionary conference at Crans, Switzerland, for an international missionary council which he considered could lead to a world League of Churches, although he did not relate that proposal to those of Constantinople or Archbishop Söderblom.

Initially, there had not been unanimity that the faith and order and life and work movements should merge. However, integration increasingly commended itself, William Temple (Archbishop of York, 1929-1942 and of Canterbury, 1942-1944) being a leading advocate and those in favour organising themselves effectively. W. A. Visser 't Hooft has pointed out that the argument for integration took on a particular momentum in the mid-1930s. This, he points out, was due to a number of factors, including the practical considerations and cost of the churches maintaining two independent movements in the midst of the depression years and the growing recognition that the separation of doctrine and practice was not a sound theological principle in itself. He comments: 'It is significant that the words which were generally picked out as the key phrase of the Oxford Conference of 1937 were, 'Let the church be the church'. Now, in the light of that rediscovery, it became increasingly clear that the primary motive in the ecumenical movement must not be to create a sense of spiritual unity between Christians or to facilitate co-operation between the churches, however important these objectives may be, but rather to demonstrate the true nature of the church in its oneness, its universality,

24. W.A. Visser 't Hooft, *The Genesis and Formation of the World Council of Churches*, op. cit., p 2

and in its apostolic and prophetic witness in the world.'[25] An increasing awareness of the world's problems as being truly global problems and of the world in the 1930s as facing a global crisis clearly demanded that the churches of the world needed to organise globally.

Following the agreement by the Edinburgh and Oxford 1937 faith and order and life and work conferences to form a World Council of Churches, further consultations led to a constitution for the new body, together with an explanatory memorandum and an invitation to join the council being sent to those churches which had received invitations to the Edinburgh and Oxford meetings. This invitation was despatched in the autumn of 1938. The position of the International Missionary Council was somewhat different from the faith and order and life and work movements in that the IMC was not directly representative of the churches, but only of missionary societies. Nonetheless, an association of the IMC with the World Council was agreed. Already in 1939, before the outbreak of World War II though amid very considerable international tensions, a provisional committee of the World Council of Churches decided to hold the first WCC assembly in 1941, but the onset of war and the resultant international chaos led to those plans being abandoned. However, although the war threw all the ecumenical plans into disarray, it also gave a further impetus to the churches' coming together in the World Council and served to underline the importance of this endeavour. The first assembly of the WCC was ultimately arranged for August 1948 in Amsterdam and, when it met, it brought together 351 official delegates of 147 churches in 44 countries. This included Orthodox representation but no Roman Catholic presence as the Vatican did not sanction participation.

The theme of Amsterdam 1948 reflected the confusion of the times as society tried to come to terms with the horror of the war and the sense of a world so at odds with God's purposes for his creation: 'Man's Disorder and God's Design'. The sections of the assembly placed the role of the church at the heart of all the discus-

25. W. A. Visser 't Hooft, *The Genesis of the World Council of Churches*, op. cit., pp.700f

sions: (1) The universal church in God's design; (2) the church's witness to God's design; (3) the church and the disorder of society; and (4) the church and the international order. The assembly's business reveals the churches searching for a clearer vision of their role in a world that had been turned upside down and was emerging from a great trauma. The experience of not one but two world wars and an economic depression of unprecedented proportions prompted the questions as to how all this fitted into what God willed for the world and as to how the church really was to respond and play its part in making the world a better place. These were profound questions indeed but the fact that the churches were now facing them together, in an ecumenical way, gave a sense of a new hope and a new opportunity to do things better. The churches, with their faith that God is continually reaching out to his creation, wanted to reach out similarly to this confused and perplexed world in which so many people had suffered in so many different ways. The church had a message, and it had a vision, and now it had a new capacity to proclaim that message and to further that vision – the capacity brought by the new fellowship of a properly established ecumenical life.

Clear intimations of such perspectives were to be found in the official message of the Amsterdam assembly. It observed that the world at the time was 'filled both with hopes and also disillusionment and despair', adding: 'Some nations are rejoicing in new freedom and power, some are bitter because freedom is denied them, some are paralysed by division, and everywhere there is an undertone of fear. There are millions who are hungry, millions who have no home, no country and no hope. Over all mankind hangs the peril of total war.' However, more positively, there was also a clear missionary vision in the official assembly message in that it recognised that because of lack of mutual correction – such lack having been caused by the disunity of the churches – the world had often heard from the churches 'not the Word of God but the words of men'. The message, therefore, prayed God to stir up the whole church to make the gospel known to the whole world, and called all people to faith and lives of Christian love and hope. It added: 'Our coming together to form a World Council

will be vain unless Christians and Christian congregations everywhere commit themselves to the Lord of the church in a new effort
to seek together, where they live, to be his witnesses and servants
among their neighbours.' The message also stressed the wider
calling of the church to promote human dignity and defend justice
and peace throughout the world. The assembly message thus had
a global missionary perspective that embraced both the traditional
call to faith as well as the more recent 'life and work' emphases.

The 1950s saw the Lund faith and order conference (1952)[26]
and the International Missionary Council meetings in Willingen
(1952) and Accra (1958); the 1960s brought the Montreal faith and
order conference (1963) and the Mexico City World Mission and
Evangelism gathering (also 1963), as well as the earlier integration
of the International Missionary Council with the WCC (New
Delhi, 1961). All of these brought important steps forward for the
churches in mission and unity matters. However, we will now
turn our specific attention to the truly historic 1962-1965 Second
Vatican Council, for with it opens up a whole new dimension to
the matters before us.

---

26. The 'Lund Principle' refers to the Lund faith and order conference's
suggestion: 'Should not our churches ask themselves ... whether they
should not act together in all matters except those in which deep differences of conviction compel them to act separately?' (cf ed O. S. Tomkins,
The Third World Conference on Faith and Order, London: SCM, 1953, p 16)

CHAPTER FIVE

Vatican II: Modern ecumenism takes full shape

The Second Vatican Council was opened by Pope John XXIII in 1962 and closed by Pope Paul VI in 1965. Until then, the Roman Catholic Church had stood very much apart from such ecumenical developments as we have surveyed here so far. This was especially clear in the response of the Vatican to the invitation to participate in the first world conference on faith and order. However, all that changed with Vatican II, which was intended by John XXIII to be the church's *aggiornamento*, its renewal and opening up and adaptation to the modern world. Behind this *aggiornamento* lay a vision of a new relationship between the church and the world. There was also the vision of a new relationship between the Roman Catholic Church and other churches – a fact witnessed by the ecumenical presence at Vatican II. Already in 1960, John XXIII had established the Secretariat for Promoting Christian Unity, under the presidency of the German Jesuit biblical scholar, Cardinal Augustin Bea. Under Bea's guidance, ecumenical observers were invited to Vatican II and, indeed, when they came to the council they played an influential role. Cardinal Franz Koenig, Archbishop of Vienna from 1956 to 1985, indicated that the success of the ecumenical observers' participation was very much Bea's achievement and that his role at Vatican II could not be rated highly enough.[1]

The council was not simply all about John XXIII. He, rather, had discerned in various currents a new mood emerging and new challenges for the church in the modern world that required new approaches. However, the visionary and prophetic John died on 3 June, 1963 and it fell to his successor, Paul VI, to open the second session of the council. Formerly Cardinal Montini, Archbishop of

---

1. *The Tablet,* 21 December 2002, as in *The National Catholic Reporter,* 7 March, 2003.

Milan, the new pope had been especially close to his predecessor, having lodged with him during the first session of the council. In his opening address to the second session, Paul VI referred to how John XXIII had convened the council 'under divine inspiration ... to open new horizons for the church'. He described the objectives of the council as 'the self-awareness of the church; its renewal; the bringing together of all Christians in unity; the dialogue of the church with the contemporary world'.[2]

Parallel to the rise of liberal Protestantism in the nineteenth and early twentieth centuries, although not without distinct differences, had been the modernist movement in the Roman Catholic Church. Both challenged traditional approaches in theological and biblical thought, embracing the critical methodology of the post-Enlightenment era. However, in 1907 Pope Pius X had formally condemned modernism in his encyclical *Pascendi Dominici Gregis* and in the Vatican decree, *Lamentabili Sane Exitu*. This conservative reaction to modernism was also witnessed in the Roman Catholic Church's social teaching, in theological instruction and in ecclesiastical appointments. Yet the more progressive thinking was not to be extinguished, even given all the might of the Vatican. It continued, notably in France where the *nouvelle théologie*, with its striking openness and positive attitude to the relationship between the church and the world, gained increasing influence in the wider church. Allied to this were the continuing biblical and liturgical movements, which in fact were affirmed by Pius XII in his encyclicals *Divino Afflante Spiritu* in 1943 and *Mediator Dei* in 1947. It was in the light of such strong and widespread currents that in 1959 Pope John XXIII announced the Second Vatican Council, to be a time of fundamental renewal for the church, a widening of its horizons. All the progressive thinking of the previous decades was to be more than vindicated in a succession of documents from Vatican II.

Fundamental to the council's teaching was its understanding of the church itself. For that reason, Vatican II's document *Lumen Gentium*, the Dogmatic Constitution on the Church, is to be seen as

---

2. As in J. D. Holmes, *The Papacy in the Modern World*, London: Burns & Oates, 1981, pp 222f

foundational in its thinking, affecting the other areas of concern to the council and not least mission and unity. Before we come to those areas as considered by Vatican II, it will therefore be necessary to give attention to *Lumen Gentium*.

From a Protestant perspective, the document simply did not go far enough, representing an under-developed ecclesiology. However, it did constitute a major step away from the former absolute exclusivism of Rome that had led to a distinct isolation. *Lumen Gentium* states: 'This Church [the one Church of Christ] constituted and organised in the world as a society, subsists in the Catholic Church, which is governed by the successor of Peter and by the bishops in communion with him, although many elements of sanctification and of truth are found outside of its visible structure. These elements, as gifts belonging to the church of Christ, are forces impelling toward catholic unity.'[3]

Such an approach clearly represented a new degree of openness to other Christians as well as an opportunity for reaching out together towards greater ecclesial unity. So, whatever about any underdeveloped understanding of the church, here was a step forward for relationships and, because of that, *Lumen Gentium* was very widely welcomed as allowing a new era of co-operation and collaboration as opposed to isolation.

Yet there were other aspects of *Lumen Gentium* that were also highly significant, not least its emphasis on the church as the pilgrim 'people of God', a dynamic departure from previously more hierarchical emphases. The council's understanding of the 'pilgrim church', on the journey from the incarnation and apostolic times to the final kingdom, thus not yet being fully perfect, opened up the theme of renewal and had clear resonances with Protestant emphases. The concept of the church's pilgrimage had already been raised by the German Roman Catholic theologian Robert Grosche in his book, *The Pilgrim Church*, and had been spoken of by Pius XII in his 1943 encyclical, *Mystici Corporis*. Now, in Vatican II, it had a fundamental importance.

Another fundamental theme in *Lumen Gentium* is the church as 'mystery'. Kevin McNamara goes so far as to describe this con-

---

3. *Lumen Gentium*, Chap 1, par 8

cept as the 'key to a unified understanding of the Constitution', adding that 'The treatment of the church as mystery has a further advantage: because of its biblical foundation and the emphasis it places on the interior element in the church, of which the Reformation tradition is so keenly aware, it has a valuable contribution to make in the field of ecumenism.'[4]

Then again, it is significant that within *Lumen Gentium*, the chapter on the hierarchy follows the chapter on the people of God and the concept of hierarchy is tempered by an emphasis on collegiality. This order in fact represents a change in the drafting stages, for in the second draft, the chapter on the hierarchy preceded a chapter on the people of God and the laity, but this was changed in the third draft. There was a real dynamic shift in the concept of the church going on here, the emphasis finally being given to the church as God's people first and then turning to the hierarchy and the laity in the two following chapters. Moreover, while *Lumen Gentium* distinguishes between priest and people, it does so in a way that stresses mutuality: 'Though they differ from one another in essence and not only in degree, the common priesthood of the faithful and the ministerial or hierarchical priesthood are nonetheless interrelated: each of them in its own special way is a participation in the one priesthood of Christ.'[5]

Lumen Gentium thus witnesses to an integrated view of the church, a conciliar vision of participation and of the role of each and all in the church's life and responsibility. Through this renewal of its life, the church would gain a new energy and vitality in carrying out its apostolic task. Here is a vision of a holy church opening itself up to the world, facing the world, engaging with the world, reaching out to the world with the message of the gospel, a missionary church.

The two documents of Vatican II that most directly address the missionary life of the church are *Ad Gentes*, The Decree on the Missionary Activity of the Church, and *Nostra Aetate*, the

---

4. Ed K. McNamara, *Vatican II: The Constitution on the Church: A theological and pastoral commentary*, London: Geoffrey Chapman, 1968, pp 56 and 76 respectively
5. *Lumen Gentium*, Ch II, par 10

Declaration on the Relation of the Church to Non-Christian Religions.

Ad Gentes

Emphasising the concept in *Lumen Gentium* of the church as 'the sacrament of salvation', *Ad Gentes* expounds the concept in terms of mission. While in the first instance it had been intended to consider mission within the scope of *Lumen Gentium*, the Constitution on the Church, considerable reaction against this led to a separate document being devoted to the subject. The very substantial nature of the final text resulted from an awareness of the tremendous growth of Roman Catholic missions and the need to give adequate treatment to the issues. Moreover, Cardinal Francis George has indicated how a further impetus towards this was the work of Protestant missiologists and the 'growing concern that human development, inculturation, and the freedom of the human person should be major concerns of mission'. George notes how these considerations in part conditioned the thinking of the Second Vatican Council when it came to say that the church by its nature is missionary.[6]

Ad Gentes views the proclamation of the gospel – preaching – as the foremost dimension of missionary outreach, drawing on the New Testament witness to the primacy of preaching the Word. Indeed, Cardinal Yves Congar, one of the drafters of *Ad Gentes*, has written that the 'implanting' of a people of God derives its origin 'first of all from the faith and thus from proclamation'.[7] However, the decree recognises that preaching is not always the approach that meets the needs of particular situations and contexts. The 'presence' of the church is already a witness and, indeed, the Eucharist itself is seen as a missionary event. Beyond this, the decree sets forth dialogue as a missionary approach. Timothy Yates writes that 'a place is given to dialogue where

6. Francis Cardinal George, *The Decree on the Church's Missionary Activity, Ad Gentes*, in ed M. L. Lambe and M. Levering, *Vatican II: Renewal within tradition*, OUP, 2008, p. 289

7. As in ibid., p 294, and Karl Muller, *Mission Theology*, Nettetal, Germany, Steyler 1987, p 43

Christians are called to familiarise themselves with national and religious traditions in order to "uncover with gladness and respect those seeds of the Word which lie hidden among them' ... At the same time, however, [Christians] are to "endeavour to illuminate these riches with the light of the gospel".'[8]

The aim in the church's mission is seen in *Ad Gentes* as the implanting of the church, as Yates has put it, through preaching, presence and dialogue, the latter two Yates describing as subordinate to the first, but all three being associated with 'a strong emphasis on service in love and the display of Christian life'.[9]

The document links missionary work with both pastoral care and Christian unity, stating: 'Thus, missionary activity among the nations differs from pastoral activity exercised among the faithful as well as from undertakings aimed at restoring unity among Christians. And yet these two ends are most closely connected with the missionary zeal because the division among Christians damages the most holy cause of preaching the gospel to every creature and blocks the way to the faith for many. Hence, by the very necessity of mission, all the baptised are called to gather into one flock, and thus they will be able to bear unanimous witness before the nations to Christ their Lord. And if they are not yet capable of bearing witness to the same faith, they should at least be animated by mutual love and esteem.'[10]

Ad Gentes thus sees the link between unity and mission in terms of the common calling of all the baptised, a united witness to Christ that, by virtue of its unity, commends the faith of the whole church. The hindrance to coming to faith caused by disunity is highlighted and this, in itself, makes the cause of Christian unity all the more imperative. For this reason, indeed, the decree provides: 'In coordination with the Secretariat for Promoting Christian Unity, let [the Congregation for the Propagation of the Faith] search out ways and means for bringing about and directing fraternal co-operation as well as harmonious living with mis-

---

8. T. Yates, *Christian Mission in the Twentieth Century*, CUP, 1994, pp 171f
9. Ibid., p 173
10. *Ad Gentes*, 6

sionary undertaking of other Christian communities, that as far as possible the scandal of division may be removed.'[11] Clearly, this requirement demonstrates a structural commitment within the Vatican to bring together missionary and ecumenical endeavours. The Vatican's 1966 *Norms* for implementing the provisions of *Ad Gentes* stated that the president of the Secretariat (now the Council) for Christian Unity was *ex officio* a member of the Sacred Congregation for the Propagation of the Faith, and the secretary of the former was co-opted to consult with the latter. Similarly, the Sacred Congregation for the Propagation of the Faith was to be represented on the Secretariat for Christian Unity.

The decree, in seeing mission as a calling shared by all the baptised, stresses how believers have the vocation to show forth, by the example of their lives and their witness, the 'new man put on at baptism' as well as the power of the Holy Spirit by which they have been strengthened when confirmed.

At the heart of this witness, for *Ad Gentes*, lies charity itself, in the fullness of its Christian sense, and so the faithful are called to care for others, following the example of Christ, the Lord of the church. The scope for ecumenical Christian witness through acts of Christian charity, through practical caring for humanity in all its diverse need, is clearly unlimited and constitutes a vital dimension in the missionary task. Through raising up congregations of faithful men and women, missionaries have a nurturing role, enabling the people of God to be a sign of God's presence in the world. *Ad Gentes* stresses that the ecumenical spirit must be nurtured in those who are brought to Christian faith. It stresses that in so far as 'religious conditions' allow, ecumenical activity should be furthered, but 'without any appearance of indifference or confusion on the one hand, or of unhealthy rivalry on the other'. Co-operation in a brotherly spirit is encouraged, according to the norms of the *Decree on Ecumenism,* so that there can be among believers 'a common profession of faith, in so far as their beliefs are common, in God and in Jesus Christ'. The decree declares: 'Let them co-operate especially for the sake of Christ, their common

---

11. Ibid., 29

Lord: let his name be the bond that unites them! This co-operation should be undertaken not only among private persons, but also, subject to approval by the local Ordinary, among churches or ecclesial communities and their works.'[12]

The positive tone and implications of *Ad Gentes* in terms of mission and ecumenism is remarkable in that it states in unmistakable terms the common calling of all the baptised. In a different document and a different context, that of relations with other faiths, *Nostra Aetate* also adopts a strikingly positive approach.

Nostra Aetate

In Vatican II's Declaration on the Relationship of the Church to Non-Christian Religions, *Nostra Aetate*, the human and religious response to the mystery of God is acknowledged in generous terms. There is both openness and freshness in the approach of the council which is clearly looking to a new future, a future entirely different from the past. The declaration starts with a recognition of the historical context of humanity, that is, the situation in which people across the globe were coming into closer contact and exchange with one another. The world had become a smaller place and the interaction of peoples from widely differing cultures and religions was a new fact of human experience, a new reality which the church simply had to recognise and on which it had to build for the future. In such a context, *Nostra Aetate* declared that 'the church examines more closely her relationship to non-Christian religions'. For the sake of promoting unity and love, Vatican II thus sought in *Nostra Aetate* to consider, first of all, what humanity holds in common and what draws people of such widely different backgrounds into fellowship.

The document sees people of all nations as possessing a profound religious sense, arising from 'a certain perception of that hidden power which hovers over the course of things and over the events of human history'. It observes how Hinduism, Buddhism and other religions are a response to a restlessness of heart, each religion in its own way and with its own teachings seeking to counter such spiritual restlessness. *Nostra Aetate* thus

---

12. Ibid., 15

proceeds to declare: 'The Catholic Church rejects nothing that is true and holy in these religions. She regards with sincere reverence those ways of conduct and of life, those precepts and teachings which, though differing in many aspects from the ones she holds and sets forth, nonetheless often reflect a ray of that Truth which enlightens all men.'

Thus, *Nostra Aetate* sets out the foundations for the Vatican II's approach to other religions in a way that creates openings for dialogue and co-operation in the future, albeit, on the church's part, 'with prudence and love and in witness to the Christian faith and life'. The document then proceeds to consider the Islamic and Jewish faiths in turn.

Acknowledging the esteem with which the Roman Catholic Church regarded Muslim people, *Nostrae Aetate* affirms how Muslims adore 'the one God ... merciful and all-powerful, the Creator of heaven and earth'. While Muslims did not acknowledge the divinity of Jesus, they nonetheless revered him as a prophet, and the Virgin Mary, the declaration stated, before reflecting on the need for reconciliation in the light of the history of the relationships between the church and the Muslim people: 'Since in the course of centuries not a few quarrels and hostilities have arisen between Christians and Moslems, this sacred synod urges all to forget the past and to work sincerely for mutual understanding and to preserve as well as to promote together for the benefit of all mankind social justice and moral welfare, as well as peace and freedom.' There was thus a clear sense in the council's deliberations that a new chapter, if not a new era, in relations between the church and Muslims should now open up, and *Nostra Aetate* gave impetus towards reconciliation and deeper mutual respect.

If such advances were now possible with regard to the Islamic faith, it was even more true with regard to Judaism. After surveying the depth of the spiritual bond that exists between Jews and Christians, on account of so much shared, biblical history, *Nostra Aetate* states: 'Since the spiritual patrimony common to Christians and Jews is thus so great, this sacred synod wants to foster and recommend that mutual understanding and respect which is the fruit, above all, of biblical and theological studies as well as of fraternal dialogues.' The council, all too aware of the curse of anti-Semitism under Hitler, went to great lengths in *Nostra Aetate* to establish the entirely unacceptable nature of any discrimination against Jewish people. However, the issue of discrimination only comes after that of the attitude towards the Jewish people in the church. The declaration first of all states that, within the church context, Jews should be regarded in a properly Christian way: 'True, the Jewish authorities and those who followed their lead pressed for the death of Christ; still, what happened in his passion cannot be charged against all the Jews, without distinction, then alive, nor against the Jews of today. Although the church is the new people of God, the Jews should not be presented as rejected or accursed by God, as if this followed from the holy scriptures. All should see to it, then, that in catechetical work or in the preaching of the word of God they do not teach anything that does not conform to the truth of the gospel and the spirit of Christ.'

Following on from this fundamental and fraternal spirit, *Nostra Aetate* addressed the issue of discrimination. It stated that any discrimination or harassment of people on account of their 'race, colour, condition of life, or religion' was reproved by the church as foreign to the mind of Christ, and added: 'On the contrary, following in the footsteps of the holy Apostles Peter and Paul, this sacred synod ardently implores the Christian faithful to "maintain good fellowship among the nations" (1 Pet 2:12), and, if possible, to live for their part in peace with all men, so that they may truly be sons of the Father who is in heaven.' It rejected all persecution and, particularly in the light of the church's shared patrimony with the Jews, decried 'hatred, persecutions, displays of anti-Semitism, directed against Jews at any time and by anyone'.

The whole thrust of *Nostra Aetate* is towards a new relationship with Judaism, Islam and other faiths through a recognition of the strivings of the human spirit towards God and the development of a new process of dialogue and interfaith collaboration.

While it is clear that in *Nostra Aetate* the Roman Catholic Church affirms all truth and holiness in other religions, equally it is committed to proclaiming Christ as 'the way and the truth and the life'. Consideration had in fact been given to including discussion of Roman Catholic-Jewish relations within the context of either the doctrine of the church or ecumenism, but for reasons of sensitivity towards Arab countries and the church's position within Arab countries, this consideration was part of the wider consideration of interfaith relations, as in *Nostra Aetate*. However, the position of this within *Nostra Aetae* comes as a high point within the document.

Arthur Kennedy, writing on *Nostra Aetate*, comments: 'The declaration promotes the recognition of points of common concern with other religions so as to establish true and authentic dialogue and understanding and to appreciate the way in which a religious sense of life is operative in shaping cultures.' Kennedy also refers to Cardinal Bea's response to the question of what the church in turns seeks from other religions. Bea writes that this is to be 'nothing more than the attitude that she herself adopts in the declaration with regard to them: namely an attitude of respect involving serious consideration of the content of her message, together with readiness to admit candidly the presence of anything good or holy ... Lastly she asks them for genuine respect for her fidelity to the mission which she is sincerely convinced she has received from Christ.'[13] This sense of mutuality in dialogue, so clearly expressed by Bea, not only set forth a new context for dialogue but also heralded a new spirit of openness, respect and charity.

It is fair to say that with Vatican II the modern ecumenical movement took its full, inclusive shape and interfaith relations found a new and firm foundation. Of course, difficulties remained in church relations, and remain, and new challenges have arisen, such as women's ordination, or the Roman Catholic Church's view that Protestant churches are not churches '*in sensu proprio*' (*Dominus Iesus*, 2000), or ethical issues not least in terms of human

---

13. Ed M. L. Lambe and M. Levering, *Vatican II: Renewal within tradition*, OUP, 2008, p 398; Augustin Cardinal Bea, *The Church and the Jewish people*, New York: Harper & Row, 1966, pp 45f

sexuality. What the full flowering of modern ecumenism has allowed, however, is an ongoing, committed dialogue in which
such challenges, or crises even, can be addressed in charity and
genuine fellowship.

CHAPTER SIX

Mission and unity from the 1970s

After the Second Vatican Council, the Roman Catholic, Orthodox and Protestant churches were on a new journey, a journey full of promise. There were to be very significant developments in both mission and unity over the following decades and we shall survey them briefly here.

Liberation theology

The Vatican Council had set the scene for major changes in the Roman Catholic Church, not least in liturgical life with the introduction of Mass in the vernacular. That very significant development, with pastoral as well as liturgical implications, in itself epitomised a whole new spirit of general openness and of engagement of the laity. It was in Latin America that all of this gave way to especially radical developments in life and mission, driven by liberation theology, drawing heavily and forthrightly on biblical insights. The context was one of a vastly predominating Roman Catholic Church set amid overwhelming poverty clashing with extremely wealthy urban elites. The Brazilian *flavelas* – whole shanty towns populated with fundamentally deprived populations – stood in stark contrast to the highly monied few, a recipe if ever for violent revolution. It was in response to such circumstances that liberation theology sought to articulate and make effective the church's witness. A key text, Gustavo Gutiérrez's *A Theology of Liberation* (1972), opened up a radical understanding of the church's responsibility not only to identify with the poor but also actively to counter poverty and oppression. In this mission, reflection and action could no longer be separated but had to be brought together to effect real change. In 1968, the Roman Catholic bishops of Latin America, meeting in Medellin, Colombia, had called for the three-fold response of analysis, reflection and action, but for Gutierrez action had to come first, primacy belonging to praxis. Another liberation theologian, Leonardo Boff, wrote about the way in which 'basic church communities', an essentially lay movement, could 'reinvent' the church. Partly arising from an institutional crisis for the church and partly as a way of bringing the church to the people, these communities were vibrant not least because of imaginative, lay pastoral leadership. Boff writes: 'Christian life in the basic communities is characterised by the absence of alienating structures, by direct relationships, by reciprocity, by a deep communion, by mutual assistance, by communality of gospel ideals, by equality among members. The specific characteristics of society are absent: rigid rules; hierarchies; prescribed relationships in a framework of a distinction of functions, qualities, and titles.' Yet, despite the revolutionary approach, which categorically called in question both celibacy and male-only ordination, Boff saw the communities not as presenting an alternative church, but as the church's 'ferment for renewal'.[1]

It was against such a background that Pope Paul VI issued his encyclical, *Evangelii Nuntiandi*. The encyclical emphatically rejected violence: 'The church cannot accept violence, especially the force of arms – which is uncontrollable once it is let loose – and indiscriminate death as the path to liberation, because she knows that violence always provokes violence and irresistibly engenders new forms of oppression and enslavement which are often harder to bear than those from which they claimed to bring freedom.'[2] However, Paul VI clearly also wanted to rein back some of the more radical theological approaches, stressing the primacy of the church's spiritual function and refusing to replace the preaching of the kingdom with a proclamation of more purely human liberation. While the basic church communities were seen as a sign of hope, dangers were highlighted in terms of challenging established church order. Subsequently, under John Paul II ecclesiastical appointments in Latin America were geared against the radical liberation theology and the then Cardinal Ratzinger, as head of

1. L. Boff, *Ecclesiogenesis*, London: Collins, 1944, pp 4 and 6
2. *Evangelii Nuntiandi*, 37

the Vatican's Congregation for the Doctrine of the Faith, enforced
more traditional teaching. From a mission perspective, *Evangelii
Nuntiandi* was positive about the aims of the liberation theologians,
if not about their theology or methods. It also emphasised the primacy of proclamation itself in missionary outreach and witnessed
to the importance of the unity of Christians: 'Indeed, if the gospel
that we proclaim is seen to be rent by doctrinal disputes, ideological polarisations or mutual condemnations among Christians, at
the mercy of the latter's differing views on Christ and the church
and even because of their different concepts of society and human
institutions, how can those to whom we address our preaching
fail to be disturbed, disoriented, even scandalised?'[3] However,
while not characterised by such a radical approach as was voiced
by the Latin American Roman Catholic liberation theologians,
Timothy Yates has pointed out how in the Anglican world writers
such as Max Warren, J. V. Taylor and Simon Barrington-Ward
also saw the significance of the small group in the mission of the
church. Yet, while in Protestant circles the life and work approach
to mission was gaining in influence, a more traditional, counter-
movement was to emerge among evangelicals, and the year 1974
was key.

The Lausanne movement

Already in 1966, the Billy Graham Evangelistic Association, in
partnership with America's *Christianity Today* magazine, had
sponsored a World Congress on Evangelism in Berlin, an assembly of 1,200 delegates from over 100 countries. It was followed by
further meetings on the theme and, ultimately, by the 1974
International Congress on World Evangelisation at Lausanne.
This Lausanne gathering – which had been called by a committee
led by Billy Graham and at which the honorary executive chairman was the Australian Anglican Bishop Jack Dain, formerly general secretary of the Australian Church Missionary Society – was
attended by over 2,300 evangelical leaders from 150 countries
with the purpose of establishing a renewed, evangelical vision of
mission. An obituary to Bishop Dain, who died in 2003, published

---

3. Ibid., 77

by the Billy Graham Foundation, indicates that while the congress had been a Billy Graham initiative, John Stott, Leighton Ford and Jack Dain had been 'the key players'.[4]

Reminiscent of Edinburgh 1910, a continuation committee was formed to carry forward the purpose of the congress. Some in the committee sought a specific focus on evangelisation, and others a more 'holistic' approach, but the committee – which styled itself the 'Lausanne Committee for World Evangelisation (Lausanne Movement)' – agreed, in a compromise formulation, to 'further the total biblical mission of the church, recognising that in this mission of sacrificial service, evangelism is primary.' The above-mentioned obituary to Bishop Dain states: 'Tensions concerning the relationship between evangelism and social responsibility surfaced more strongly at the first meeting of the continuation committee held in Mexico City. Billy Graham favoured restricting the commitment to evangelism only. John Stott, in a gracious but firm intervention, pressed for both to be included. It was a tense encounter and Dain made a powerful and timely advocacy for the broader agenda. The Lausanne spirit led to further related international conferences which produced a range of position papers on issues relevant to global mission.

A lasting inspiration of Lausanne 1974 was the Lausanne Covenant, a comprehensive, evangelical statement setting forth the commitment and rationale behind the stated aim of taking 'the whole gospel to the whole world', a slogan highly evocative of the turn of the century watchword, 'The evangelisation of the world in this generation'. The covenant, which had been drafted by John Stott, was affirmed on the final day of the congress and was signed by Billy Graham and Bishop Dain.

After affirming that the gospel is for the whole world, and expressing determination to proclaim the gospel 'to all mankind and to make disciples of every nation', the Lausanne Covenant affirmed the sovereignty of God's will and purpose and expressed a new dedication to making the gospel known. From the very opening sentences, the text is unambiguously evangelical and evangelistic in tenor. Its approach to scripture is a classic formulation:

---

4. http://www.wheaton.edu/bgc/archives/dainmemories.html

'We affirm the divine inspiration, truthfulness and authority of both Old and New Testament scriptures in their entirety as the only written word of God, without error in all that it affirms, and the only infallible rule of faith and practice.' On the 'Uniqueness and Universality of Christ', the covenant not only states that everyone has some knowledge of God, but goes on to reject 'as derogatory to Christ and the gospel every kind of syncretism and dialogue which implies that Christ speaks equally through all religions and ideologies ... Jesus Christ has been exalted above every other name; we long for the day when every knee shall bow to him and every tongue shall confess him Lord.' Nonetheless, dialogue is affirmed in the covenant, when its purpose is to listen sensitively in order to understand others.

The authors well aware of the thrust of the life and work movement, the Lausanne Covenant affirms that evangelism and sociopolitical involvement are both part of Christian duty. Strikingly calling for Christians to break out of their ecclesiastical ghettos and to 'permeate non-Christian society', the covenant goes on to affirm co-operation in evangelism: 'Evangelism also summons us to unity, because our oneness strengthens our witness, just as our disunity undermines our gospel of reconciliation.' The concept here is of those who share 'the same biblical faith' being closely united in fellowship, work and witness; the covenant contains the pledge to seek 'a deeper unity in truth, worship, holiness and mission'.

The realities of missionary life are readily recognised in the Lausanne Covenant, which acknowledges how the dominant role of western missions had been fast disappearing. It also speaks with hope of the younger churches as vital to the task of world evangelisation, and of the global mission as bearing fruit through a growing partnership among the churches.

While recognising the need for new efforts towards world evangelisation, the covenant also shows a keen awareness of both social responsibility and development issues: 'Missionaries should flow ever more freely from and to all six continents in a spirit of humble service. The goal should be, by all available means and at the earliest possible time, that every person will have the opportunity to hear, understand, and to receive the good news. We cannot hope to attain this goal without sacrifice. All of us are shocked by the poverty of millions and disturbed by the injustices which cause it. Those of us who live in affluent circumstances accept our duty to develop a simple lifestyle in order to contribute more generously to both relief and evangelism.' Then again, the covenant states clearly that the gospel 'does not presuppose the superiority of any culture to another, but evaluates all cultures according to its own criteria of truth and righteousness'.

In the same way as Edinburgh 1910 had considered the whole area of the relations between missions and governments, so also the Lausanne Covenant reminds the world that every government has the duty, as appointed by God, to secure conditions of peace, justice and liberty in which the church can live out its worship and witness without let or hindrance. The covenant affirms, however, that worldwide evangelism can only be possible as the Holy Spirit renews the church 'in truth and wisdom, faith, holiness, love and power'.

It is clear that while the thrust of the Lausanne Covenant is certainly in the evangelistic direction, it also contains clear evidence that some of the lessons that had been learned about mission in the International Missionary Council and the World Council of Churches had not gone unrecognised in the specifically evangelical constituency. There are nuanced qualifications in the covenant that show a wider awareness. However, it is also clear that the Lausanne spirit was definitely at odds with the tendency in the WCC to understand mission in a broader sense. The language of world evangelisation distinctly echoed Edinburgh 1910 in a way that was not found in the WCC.

Lausanne 1974 led on to international, evangelical missionary conferences in Pattaya, Thailand (1980), Manila (1989, Lausanne II) and Pattaya (2004). Kenneth Ross comments: 'This movement understands itself to be maintaining the priority that the Edinburgh conference gave to evangelism when the WCC, in [the Lausanne movement's] view, has often been preoccupied with other concerns. While institutionally there is a direct line of continuity from the Edinburgh Conference to the World Council of Churches, there are mission movements outside the WCC that understand themselves to represent more faithfully the spirit and focus of Edinburgh 1910.'[5]

The issue facing contemporary ecumenism is the need to bring together what are now clearly two distinct trajectories in mission history, and indeed the 2010 conferences at Edinburgh and Cape Town (Lausanne III) tend to suggest precisely this division. However, there have been some very hopeful signs that the 'ecumenical' and the 'evangelical' strands are coming together. In the 1990s momentum grew towards the establishment of a new and much more inclusive Global Christian Forum, leading to its first meeting in Nairobi in 2007. The Global Christian Forum says it is about 'bringing into conversation with one another Christians and churches from very different traditions who have little or never talked to each other. It is about building bridges where there are none, overcoming prejudices, creating and nurturing new relationships.'[6]

The 2007 Nairobi meeting brought together 226 leaders and representatives of all the main Christian traditions in the world – Protestant (including Anglican), Roman Catholic, Evangelical, Holiness, Independent, Orthodox (Eastern and Oriental) and Pentecostal. Participation was truly global, coming from Africa, Asia, the Caribbean, Europe, Latin America, the Middle East, North America and the Pacific. It was addressed by three key speakers: Samuel Kobia, then general secretary of the World Council of Churches, who spoke about the unprecedented breadth of the participation; and Pentecostal theologians Wonsuk Ma from Korea and Cheryl Johns from the United States, who addressed the issues of unity and mission. While acknowledging certain shortcomings in the event – in particular, the fact that the time for Bible study in small groups was too limited, a lack of representation from the Global South in the leadership of the assembly, and imbalances in terms of certain groups (age, gender, disabilities, indigenous groups) – the Forum describes the unique-

5. K. R. Ross, *Edinburgh 2010: Springboard for Mission*, Pasadena, California: William Carey International University Press, 2009, p 27
6. http://www.globalchristianforum.org/

ness of the Nairobi meeting: 'The gathering was characterised by a remarkable spirit of openness and eagerness to listen to one another and break down barriers. As the momentum built up there was a growing awareness among the participants of being part of an extraordinary and "historic" event. The participatory and flexible style of the meeting helped to create numerous opportunities for conversation and mutual discovery. For many of the representatives of the churches and organisations involved in the ecumenical movement it was a unique occasion to interact with such a powerful group of evangelicals and pentecostals, and vice-versa.[7] The message from the gathering affirmed the ongoing nature of the process and invited yet others to participate in the future. In many ways reminiscent of the tactical approach of Edinburgh 1910, however, potentially divisive issues were avoided at Nairobi but, rather, the sharing of 'faith journeys' as the basis for discussion was a creative way forward in the circumstances.

Then again, as illustrative of a more inclusive approach, participation in the council preparing for the marking of the centenary of Edinburgh 1910 was similarly comprehensive. Speaking in 2009, the newly appointed general secretary of the World Council of Churches, Olav Fykse Tveit, referred to the importance of building 'new bridges to other churches in the Global Christian Forum' and to all as sharing the goal of 'holistic and healing mission'.[8]

The World Council of Churches: Assemblies, 1968-2006
The World Council of Churches from the 1960s and 1980s tried to hold together the political and the missionary emphases, but it was a difficult balance.

The Uppsala assembly of 1968 led to the establishment of the WCC's Programme to Combat Racism and the Commission on the Churches' Participation in Development, leaving the council's Unit II, 'Justice and Service' as its largest department. While the

---

7. http://www.globalchristianforum.org/nairobi/
8. http://www.oikoumene.org/en/resources/documents/central-committee/geneva-2009/reports-and-documents/speech-by-olav-fykse-tveit-to-the-wcc-central-committee.html

assembly declared that 'churches need a new openness to the world in its aspirations, its achievements, its restlessness and its despair', it also stated that all church structures had to be examined against the criterion of enabling the church and its members to be in mission, calling equally both for more dialogue with the world and more effective proclamation of the gospel. The message of the assembly, noting the turbulence of the times, called for the ecumenical movement to become 'bolder, and more representative'. Already at Uppsala, an assembly characterised by political engagement, there was an awareness of the structural limitations arising from the make-up of the membership of the council itself.[9]

Timothy Yates has noted how the 1975 Nairobi assembly of the WCC saw a certain *rapprochement* towards the evangelical constituency. He refers to Bishop Mortimer Arias' address, affirming world evangelisation as the primary calling of the church and drawing on the Lausanne Congress and Roman Catholic insights, as reassuring evangelicals and as setting a different tone from what David Edwards had called the 'secularising radicals' of Uppsala.[10] Nonetheless, Nairobi did represent a certain theological consolidation of the Uppsala direction and the Programme to Combat Racism and its controversial special fund were affirmed, the search for a 'just, participatory and sustainable society' becoming a major theme. The assembly's report on 'Confessing Christ Today' evidenced a rather liberal, if somewhat nuanced, approach: '(61) Evangelism cannot be delegated to either gifted individuals or specialised agencies. It is entrusted to the 'whole church', the body of Christ, in which the particular gifts and functions of all members are but expressions of the life of the whole body. (62) This wholeness must take expression in every particular cultural, social, and political context. Therefore, the evangelisation of the world starts at the level of the congregation, in the local and ecumenical dimension of its life: worship, sacrament, preaching, teaching and healing, fellowship and service, witnessing in life and in death.'[11]

9. Cf *The Uppsala Report 1968*, WCC Geneva 1968, p 5f and ad loc
10. T. Yates, *Christian Mission in the Twentieth Century*, CUP 1994, p 219
11. Ed D. M. Paton, *Breaking Barriers*: Nairobi 1975, London: SPCK, Grand Rapids: Wm B. Eerdmans, 1976, p 53

The 1983 Vancouver assembly of the WCC conceived of mission very much in terms of 'witenssing', with a major agenda item titled 'Witnessing in a Divided World'. In considering the context of witnessing, that is, contemporary and local cultures, the report of this part of the assembly balanced the acknowledgement that culture holds communities together and to a large extent defines communities with a recognition that not all culture is necessarily good. The report affirmed culture in a concise yet comprehensive way: 'It is preserved in language, thought patterns, ways of life, attitudes, symbols and presuppositions, and is celebrated in art, music, drama, literature and the like. It constitutes the collective memory of the people and the collective heritage which will be handed down to generations still to come.' All of this was seen as good and, in a real sense, expressing something fundamental about the created order. Yet the report went on to point out how each culture possesses those elements that 'deny life and oppress people', and even declared certain forms of religious culture and sub-cultures as 'demonic' on account of their manipulative and life-denying tendencies. The cultural aspect of missionary activity was recognised, in which culture can be so bound up with proclamation that the whole witness can be jeopardised as new and different cultures are encountered. The assembly was keen not only to assist the churches to reflect on such matters, but also to assist the various cultural expressions of Christianity to engage with each other.[12]

This part of the Vancouver assembly also highlighted three areas of missionary concern: witnessing among children, the poor and people of living faiths. All of these concerns, no doubt, contributed to a major programme that was launched at Vancouver: 'Justice, peace and the integrity of creation'. The basis of this programme was distinctly evangelical in the broadest sense of the term, for it was seen very much as 'witness'. In stressing that evangelism should undergird the work in all WCC programmes, the report of the assembly's programme guidelines committee stated three very significant ways in which the council could as-

---

12. Ed D. Gill, *Gathered for Life, The Official report of the VI Assembly of the World Council of Churches*, Geneva: WCC, 1983, pp 32f

sist the evangelistic work of the churches: by helping the churches to understand better the interplay between gospel and culture;
by seeking to develop dialogue with the evangelical constituency
not associated with the WCC; and by helping to clarify the distinction between evangelism and proselytism.[13]

The awareness of the wider Christian world – quite apart from
Rome and Orthodoxy – thus featured clearly in the Vancouver assembly's thinking, and only two years later the council appointed
a South American Evangelical Methodist as its new general secretary, Emilio Castro, a former president of his denomination in
Uruguay (1970-72). Lesslie Newbigin wrote of the charismatic
Castro: 'From the moment that I first met Emilio Castro and heard
him speak, I was drawn to him by his rare combination of qualities that, in others, so often fall apart: a glowing assurance about
the gospel and a corresponding desire to share it, a burning com-
passion for the victims of public wrong, a pastoral care for individual people and a bubbling sense of humour ... Apart from all
his other achievements, I think that *Mission and Evangelism – An
Ecumenical Affirmation* will stand as a great symbol of what he has
achieved. More than any other document that I have read from
any quarter, it seems to me to say what needs to be said on these
much debated issues. I am sure that it would not have been produced had it not been for the quality of leadership that Emilio has
given so steadily throughout these ten years.'[14] *Mission and
Evangelism - An Ecumenical Affirmation* was a 1982 WCC document which precisely affirmed the twin stated themes, issued at
the time when Dr Castro was director of the WCC's Commission
on World Mission and Evangelism. It was significant in that it addressed a perceived divide, in a way that the Vancouver assembly
also did in its own way.

Canberra was the venue for the WCC's 1991 assembly which
took as its theme, 'Come, Holy Spirit – Renew the Whole
Creation'. The assembly opened three weeks after the Gulf war
broke out, to drive Iraq out of Kuwait, and tensions mounted as a

---

13. Ibid., p 254
14. *Emilio Castro: Servant of World Mission and Evangelism*, in *The
International Review of Mission* 73, 289 (January), p 110

result of differing perspectives among the churches' representatives on the subject of war itself. Quite apart from this issue, however, the Orthodox participants were to express very serious concerns indeed, not least about the future direction of the ecumenical movement. The Orthodox saw the council as increasingly departing from its stated Basis, that is: 'The World Council of Churches is a fellowship of churches which confess the Lord Jesus Christ as God and Saviour according to scriptures and therefore seek to fulfill together their common calling to the glory of the one God, Father, Son and Holy Spirit.' The departure, the Orthodox sensed, was evidenced in the lack of a proper priority for faith and order issues. A statement from the Orthodox participants indicated: 'The tendency to marginalise the Basis in WCC work has created some dangerous trends in the WCC. We miss from many WCC documents the affirmation that Jesus Christ is the world's Saviour. We perceive a growing departure from biblically-based Christian understanding of: (a) the trinitarian God; (b) salvation; (c) the 'good news' of the gospel itself ; (d) human beings as created in the image and likeness of God; and (e) the church, among others ... Our hope is that the results of Faith and Order work will find a more prominent place in the various expressions of the WCC, and that tendencies in the opposite direction will not be encouraged.'[15] There were also concerns about the integrity of Christian witness in interfaith dialogue and about too loose an understanding of the 'Spirit'. Given that the theme of the assembly focused on the work of the Holy Spirit, the Orthodox clearly felt that there was not a sufficiently faithful understanding of pneumatology, which they said was inseparable from christology or the doctrine of the Trinity.

There was also considerable controversy in the Church of Ireland over the Canberra meeting. The Presbyterian Church in Ireland had already in 1980 withdrawn from membership of the WCC, a major factor in that decision having been the activities of the council's Programme to Combat Racism and in particular grants to the Patriotic Front in the then Rhodesia, news of which had come at the same time as reports of the murder of several

15. http:/ /www.orthodoxinfo.com/ecumenism/ canberra_1991.aspx?

Northern Ireland missionaries in that country. However, there were also underlying conservative theological trends in Irish Presbyterianism that were at variance with theological approaches typically found in WCC circles. Now, in 1991, some in the Church of Ireland, belonging to the Church Society, published a leaflet not only attacking the lack of an adequate report in the 1991 General Synod Book of Reports (although this was most likely simply a timing issue, as the General Synod was held in the May following the February Canberra assembly), but also going on to launch a catalogue of deeply felt complaints, drawing heavily on the testimony of the outspoken English churchman, Archdeacon George Austin: lack of democracy and the dominating voice of 'North American liberals'; the 'political bias' of many representatives at Canberra regarding the Gulf war, who focused not on the record of Saddam Hussein but on what was termed 'Western imperialism'; 'heretical' teaching about the Spirit; and radical feminism.

In particular, fears about departing from the Basis had been compounded by a dramatic presentation at the Canberra assembly by Professor Chung from Korea, who had burnt a list of martyrs during her speech on the relationship of the Holy Spirit to the spirits of those who had died in anger, resentment, bitterness and grief, and declaring that it was through those ancestor spirits that Koreans heard the voice of the Holy Spirit. In a substantial response to the Church Society at the 1992 Church of Ireland General Synod, the Church Unity Committee acknowledged the range of concerns, including Professor Chung's 'undoubtedly provocative and controversial' presentation and speech, while at the same time re-affirming the Church of Ireland's commitment to the WCC, dismissing calls for Church of Ireland withdrawal as unhelpfully 'obstructionist'.[16]

Such controversy illustrates a continuing theological division at the time between conservatives and liberals, evangelicals and ecumenists, but from the perspective of mission the Canberra assembly did see one major advance – the joining into membership of the WCC of the China Christian Council. That, in itself, was a consider-

---

16. cf General Synod of the Church of Ireland, Reports 1992, pp 246-250

able sign of hope at a time of real division and perhaps even perplexity about the future of the ecumenical movement itself.

The 50th anniversary year of the World Council of Churches, 1998, was marked by its eighth assembly, in Harare, Zimbabwe. As is the case with any major anniversary, it was an occasion to take stock, and a basic text for this exercise was the document, *Towards a Common Understanding and Vision of the World Council of Churches* (known in abbreviation as CUV), which had been agreed in the previous year by the council's central committee. For this document, the 1950 Toronto Statement, which set out to define the WCC's competence and scope, remained foundational: the WCC was not a 'superchurch'; it did not negotiate church unions; it did not have one single ecclesiological understanding; membership did not mean an acceptance of any 'relativism'; and nor did membership entail any particular understanding of church unity. The CUV document recognised, however, that while Toronto remained foundational, ecumenical experience and understanding had deepened over the intervening years; indeed, it hardly could have been otherwise when one considers all the developments. For that reason, CUV in particular brought to the fore an understanding of the WCC as 'ecclesiological challenge', noting that the concept of the council as a 'fellowship' at least suggested 'that the Council is more than a mere functional association of churches set up to organise activities in areas of common interest'.[17] The document also noted how the ecumenical movement, over the course of the precious decade, had provided a definite impetus for the emergence of new Christian communities and movements, mainly flexible in nature and constitution but having become important partners with the WCC, especially through the 'justice, peace and integrity of creation' issues. CUV also recognised how many such movements had been truly prophetic, both within and outside the established churches, allowing new dimensions of Christian witness and service.

The Harare assembly's main themes lacked a particularly strong mission emphasis, however, focusing on membership and

---

17. *Towards a Common Understanding and Vision of the World Council of Churches*, par 3.2

relationships, issues of global concern such as debt and globalis-
ation and, understandably, the African situation and the
HIV / Aids crisis. The assembly itself followed a celebration marking the end of the ecumenical decade, 'Churches in Solidarity
with Women'. The assembly's section on church relationships
dealt with Orthodox reservations, approving the creation of a
special commission to devote at least three years to studying the
issues related to the participation of Orthodox in the WCC and to
present proposals to the central committee. The idea of a forum of
Christian churches and ecumenical organisations was discussed,
the concept having been developed at an earlier, broadly based
consultation in 1998. It received endorsement by the assembly, although there was some concern about what the precise nature of
such a forum would be, the need being felt to distinguish between
a looser gathering of church representatives and the accountability
and commitment involved in WCC membership.

'Witness' was a sub-theme of one of the three 'units' in which
the business of the assembly was conducted, addressing the issues of evangelism and proselytism. However, a declaration from
evangelical participants at Harare stated: 'While the theme, "Turn
to God – Rejoice in Hope", should have led to a strong emphasis
on mission, evangelism and the church, this was largely missing.
Work in these areas by member churches and the WCC ... was not
drawn in. We urge a renewed emphasis on mission and evangelism which will empower the churches to communicate the gospel
through the world. Christ's transforming gospel both affirms and
critiques cultures and societies, and requires humility, sensitivity
and prophetic engagement with oppression.'[18] The statement
was a frank observation and went on to affirm that, in order for
there to be meaningful evangelical participation in the WCC, the
council would have to give more emphasis to the biblical, christo-
centric and missionary emphasis of its original vision.

Preaching during the Harare assembly, the then Archbishop
of Canterbury, the evangelical George Carey, contrasted what he
described as the western church's preoccupation with single issues, sapping the church's energy, with the vitality of African

18. http://www.wcc-coe.org/wcc/assembly/or-8g-e.html

Christianity. He said that for much of the twentieth century, the western church, especially in Europe, had accepted an inevitability of decline, but he challenged such an outlook, concluding with a ringing confidence in outreach: 'Christ must be the heartbeat of our preaching, our living, our social work and our concern for justice and peace. And only when we walk in his light we will find that our crisis will become our opportunity for growth and source of confidence for the future. And that's why the WCC message is so right: Turn to God, rejoice in hope.'[19] It was a brave attempt to inject an evangelical perspective, but his approach was not a characteristic feature in an essentially liberal and largely politically driven agenda, including the politics of global church relations and the structure of the council itself.

The report of the WCC general secretary, Konrad Raiser, to the Harare assembly focused, like the agenda, on church relationships, the council itself and the 'ecumenical jubilee', and the global context. Mission was hardly mentioned by Raiser, and evangelism not at all. Therein was symbolised a real division in Christianity, a division which the Harare assembly approached somewhat reluctantly, or at least with some hesitations. Yet Raiser did sound a particularly prophetic note when he said that, in not returning to Amsterdam for the 50th anniversary meeting of the WCC, but in going to Harare, the council had wanted to signal how it was looking forwards, not backwards. Raiser noted how regions like Africa and Latin America would, in the years ahead, have a special influence in shaping the future of Christianity and the ecumenical movement itself. Yet, while it is true that those regions have seen immense growth in the church, the formal ecumenical movement is only now beginning to come to terms with the need for a new structure, and Christianity itself is dividing quite markedly between the global north and the global south, as well as within both regions, in terms of liberal versus traditional theological perspectives. It is precisely in that division that a real challenge faces church relations today, and Raiser did foresee that in his own way. However, it is somewhat ironic that the Harare assembly was so

---

19. WCC Eighth Assembly Press Release No 48: Sermon at the Anglican Church of St Mary and All Saints in Harare, 13 December, 1998

'light' on mission and evangelism when Africa was precisely a place of such immense opportunity for proclamation and church growth.

The 2006 Porto Alegre assembly adopted the document *Called to be the One Church*, which had in part the purpose of inviting the churches into a renewed conversation about the quality and degree of their fellowship and communion, and about the issues which still divided them. The document reaffirmed that the churches in membership of the WCC remained committed to the goal of full visible unity, stating: 'The catholicity of the church expresses the fullness, integrity, and totality of its life in Christ through the Holy Spirit in all times and places. This mystery is expressed in each community of baptised believers in which the apostolic faith is confessed and lived, the gospel is proclaimed, and the sacraments are celebrated. Each church is the church catholic and not simply a part of it. Each church is the church catholic, but not the whole of it. Each church fulfils its catholicity when it is in communion with the other churches. We affirm that the catholicity of the church is expressed most visibly in sharing holy communion and in a mutually recognised and reconciled ministry.'[20]

Called to be the One Church thus had not only a traditional vision of church unity but also expressed that vision in dynamic terms, going on to stress the themes of interactivity, mutual accountability and reconciliation. The document also spoke of mission as 'integral' to the church's life, but set this very much in the context of dialogue with other faiths: since the churches found themselves living alongside other faiths and ideologies, they were called to 'dialogue and collaboration'.[21]

Although evangelism may not have figured particularly highly in the Porto Alegre agenda, it was the focus of the (Bossey) Ecumenical Institutes's first study seminar after the assembly. The seminar, which built on the work of the 2005 conference on world mission and evangelism in Athens and the 2006 WCC Porto Alegre assembly, was entitled, 'Towards a New Ecumenical

---

20. *Called to be the One Church*, II, 6
21. Ibid., IV, 11

Agenda on Evangelism in the 21st Century', and highlighted key themes and issues for ecumenical co-operation in evangelism. The participants noted how there were churches that were strongly committed to evangelism, growing new churches and fostering renewal movements, and churches in decline and stagnation in terms of evangelism. Equally, it was noted how many churches with great capacity for forwarding mission and evangelism required ecumenical assistance. There were opportunities for sharing resources and sharing enthusiasm itself. The seminar reported, with considerable insight: 'Ecumenical co-operation in evangelism should regain a high and visible priority in the working structure and study programme of the WCC in the post-Porto Alegre period. We are convinced that approaching the 100th anniversary of the world mission conference in Edinburgh in the year 2010 a common commitment to recapture the passion for evangelism for the future generation of ecumenical and church leaders lies at the heart of the ecumenical purpose altogether. On the other hand, without giving evangelism a proper priority and prominent place in the work of the WCC, the urgently needed broader ecumenical approach and collaboration with non-member churches in both the Pentecostal and charismatic, and the evangelical tradition (which is also a driving force behind proposals for a Global Christian Forum) would be hindered in the future. A common concern for evangelism is a key theme and a strategic bridge for ecumenical co-operation between WCC member churches and the majority of non-member churches in the 21st century.'[22]

Commission on World Mission and Evangelism
The 2005 conference on world mission and evangelism, held in Athens, has been mentioned. As recorded earlier, the International Missionary Council merged with the WCC at the council's 1961 New Delhi assembly, which gave rise to the WCC's Commission on World Mission and Evangelism (CWME). We shall consider briefly the significance of the CWME's series of con-

---

22. http://habitusnetwork.org/ecumenism/bossey-first-ecumenical-study-seminar-after-porto-alegre-3.html

ferences which, in fact, stand in line from Edinburgh 1910. We have considered the significance of New Delhi itself and the Mexico City conference of 1963. There have been five since then: Bangkok 1972/73, Melbourne 1980, San Antonio 1989, Salvador da Bahia 1996, and Athens 2005. (The world mission conferences from Edinburgh 1910 to New Delhi, before the establishment of the CWME, were Jerusalem 1928, Tambaram 1938, Whitby 1947, Willingen 1952 and Achimota/Accra 1958, and have been referred to above.)

Bangkok 1972/73: At this gathering, with its striking theme, 'Salvation Today', but quite wide-ranging concept of mission itself in terms of both socio-political concerns and the individual, there was a significant move to assert the independence of the younger churches and their partnership with the traditionally dominant western churches. This was felt to the extent that it was suggested that the latter should withdraw from any dominant role. In this way, a genuinely global mission was envisaged and, in many ways, Bangkok marks a major step towards such equalisation, not least with its emphasis on contextual theology and recognising cultural identities. Those present had grappled with the issues of exploitation and injustice not only in the affairs of the world but also in terms of church relationships. However, there was considerable feeling among evangelicals that the conference had not, in fact, developed a sufficiently clear theology of salvation and that, at root, it was heavily biased towards socio-political engagement. Bernard Ott, reflecting on the conference some thirty years later, concluded that its approach signalled the need to continue mission work 'in the biblical, evangelical sense' in co-operation alongside those missions with a clear commitment to world evangelisation.[23]

Melbourne 1980: Under the influence of liberation theology, this conference was deeply committed to the role of the poor – and the poorer churches of the world – in the mission task, but it also

---

23. B. Ott, *Beyond Fragmentation: Integrating Mission and Theological Education – A Critical Assessment of Some Recent Developments in Evangelical Theological Education*, Oxford *et al*: Regnum Books International, 2001, p 75

gave place to the theme of evangelism. Coming after the emergence of the evangelical Lausanne movement, the conference sought to effect some reconciliation between the liberal and conservative approaches to mission. The thrust of the conference's deliberations was reflected in the 1982 WCC document, *Mission and Evangelism – An Ecumenical Affirmation*, which provided a considered view of the theme of conversion itself, emphasising both its corporate and individual significance: 'The call to conversion, as a call to repentance and obedience, should also be addressed to nations, groups and families. To proclaim the need to change from war to peace, from injustice to justice, from racism to solidarity, from hate to love is a witness rendered to Jesus Christ and to his kingdom. The prophets of the Old Testament addressed themselves constantly to the collective conscience of the people of Israel calling the rulers and the people to repentance and to renewal of the covenant ... The experience of conversion gives meaning to people in all stages of life, endurance to resist oppression, and assurance that even death has no final power over human life because God in Christ has already taken our life with him, a life that is "hidden with Christ in God". (Col 3:3)'[24]

San Antonio 1989: The conference at San Antonio has become especially associated with its articulation of the relationship of Christianity to other religions, a constant issue in mission thinking. However, San Antonio did reach a degree of consensus on the issue when it recognised that the church could not point anywhere other than to Christ as the way of salvation, nor could God be limited in his saving power; the tension here was affirmed although there was no final resolution of the issue. Nonetheless, the conference had achieved an effective statement of how things stood between liberals and conservatives, in a way that was honest and could appeal to those who embraced either approach. Moreover, the theme of the San Antonio conference, 'Your will be done: Mission in Christ's way', displayed in its own terms an incarnational emphasis that itself sought to bring together the differing approaches to mission. Darrell Guder has commented: 'The

---

24. *Mission and Evangelism – An Ecumenical Affirmation*, Geneva: WCC, 1982, ad loc

emphasis upon incarnational evangelism emerged in various attempts to define the church's witness in ways that sought to include both verbal proclamation and social witness.'[25]

Salvador da Bahia 1996: A return to an important theme at Bangkok, the interrelationship of gospel and culture, was a marked feature of the Salvador da Bahia conference. Two developments had led to a sense that the church needed to return to the topic: the geopolitical shift that had taken place with the collapse of communism and the Soviet Union and the emergence of cultural and ethnic factors in conflict. There is no doubt that the model of gospel and culture that obtained in 1910 was very much that of replicating the church at home (in the west) with the church in the mission field. Gospel and western culture went together and the communication of the gospel was seen as having its part in promoting civilisation itself. However, such an approach belonged to distant history by the time of the Salvador da Bahia conference which, nonetheless, affirmed that the church had to affirm but also critique and challenge cultural expression.

Athens 2005: The conference issued a letter to the Christian world calling on the churches to be 'healing and reconciling communities of hope, open to all'. The Athens conference, as its letter to the churches evidenced, clearly understood the subtleties of differing approaches to mission, expressing the situation well when it described the missionary character of the church as having greater diversity than ever before, being characterised by differing and distinctive responses to the gospel. The conference recognised that this diversity could be unsettling, but nonetheless saw the Holy Spirit at work in it. Athens 2005 recognised that, while the centres of power were in the global north, it was the churches in the global south that were growing most rapidly, 'as a result of faithful Christian mission and witness'.

---

25. D. Guder, *Incarnation and the Church's Evangelistic Mission*, in ed P. W. Chilcote and L. C. Warner, *The Study of Evangelism: Exploring a Missional Practice of the Church*, Grand Rapids and Cambridge: W. B. Eerdmans, 2008, p 172

Bilateral and multilateral church relationships

The Second Vatican Council opened the way for further advances in ecumenical understanding through dialogue during the subsequent decades. In ecumenical terms, this was seen in the development of a whole raft of bilateral theological dialogues with other world communions, in the Faith and Order Commission of the World Council of Churches, and in interfaith discussions. The inter-church dialogues have ranged from discussions towards the organic union of churches to those that do not have such a specific goal but, rather, are geared towards greater mutual understanding and establishing common aspects of the Christian faith. However, a feature of all these dialogues, as Mary Tanner has pointed out, is mission as their motivating force. Speaking at an ecumenical study day in Ireland in 2007, she commented in this connection: 'There is hardly a document that does not give as its rationale the absolute requirement to be together for the sake of the mission of the church.' Moreover, on the same occasion, she referred to the 'spiritual experience of dialogue', pointing to how the very exercise of engaging in interchurch dialogue itself deepens relationships and fellowship, and quoting, as an example, from the Anglican-Roman Catholic International Commission's report, *Church as Communion*: 'The members of the commission have not only been engaged in theological dialogue. Their work and study have been rooted in shared prayer and common life. This in itself has given them a profound experience of communion in Christ; not indeed that full sacramental communion which is our goal, but nevertheless a true foretaste of that fullness of communion for which we pray and strive.'[26]

However, Mary Tanner also pointed out in her lecture that a 'burning question' arises in relation to the inter-church dialogues that have been in process for decades now: 'Put crudely, it is – "So what?" What is the result of all of this conversation, all of this advance in understanding and real friendship between the privileged few? Is the conversation making any practical difference? ... Are the theological dialogues in fact becoming obstacles, simply

26. Dame Mary Tanner, address to the Irish Inter-Church Meeting's study day, Emmaus Retreat Centre, Swords, 24 October, 2007

delaying tactics for those who don't want to lose their own identity and are happy to pile up more and more topics for discussion?' In response, she challenged the churches to develop more effective ways of responding to the fruits of the dialogues, an issue which she said pointed to the deeper issue of 'authority, or the lack of it' in the churches.

The modern ecumenical movement has, however, seen certain very significant advances in the restoration of communion between certain churches. The 1947 establishment of the Church of South India brought together, for the first time, episcopal and non-episcopal churches – the Anglican Church of India, Burma and Ceylon, the Methodist Church and the South India United Church (Presbyterian, Congregationalist and Dutch Reformed). The union was based on the 1919 Tanquebar Manifesto which had remarkable similarities to the Lambeth Quadrilateral in the latter's stating of the fundamentals of Anglicanism in relation to scripture, the creeds, the sacraments and the historic episcopate. The Church of North India, established in 1970, was a similar model.

Writing in 2003 following the completion of the first three years of a relationship of full communion between The Episcopal Church, USA and the Evangelical Lutheran Church in America, Bishop Christopher Epting of The Episcopal Church described the sharing in episcopal ordination liturgies in both churches as often having been 'a powerful experience for bishops and has led to a new sense of communion between synods and dioceses'. Indeed, the foundational document for this relationship – which was not a 'merger' of the two denominations, but a new relationship of communion – was entitled *Called to Common Mission*. Bishop Epting wrote that some people had suggested that co-operative efforts in mission that had been developed over the first three years of communion could have been initiated without the special relationship. However, he countered that it had been the relationship of full communion that had in fact inspired common mission strategies.[27] The Episcopal Church's 2009 General Convention overwhelmingly approved the move to establish full

27. *The Living Church*, 15 June 2003

communion between The Episcopal Church and the Northern and Southern Provinces of the Moravian Church.

The establishing of full communion between the Nordic/ Baltic Lutheran churches and the Anglican churches in Britain and Ireland, under the 1995 Porvoo Common Statement, was another earlier advance, and the 1988 Meissen Agreement between the German Protestant Church and the Church of England, while not establishing full communion, was a decisive step towards the deepening of relations. Quite apart from such steps in ecclesial reconciliation, the twentieth century saw the establishment of numerous national councils of churches, with close links to the Roman Catholic Church and some even with full Roman Catholic membership.

CHAPTER SEVEN

From Edinburgh 1910 to Mission 2010

The story of Edinburgh 1910 and its fruits, in terms of subsequent missionary work and the development of ecumenical life throughout the twentieth century, leads to the inevitable question as to what lessons are to be learned from the past century.

The past that we have surveyed has revealed many initiatives flowing from the Edinburgh 1910 event, both in terms of missionary organisation, planning and outreach and of new relationships between churches and world communions. The themes of mission and unity have come together in real and significant ways over the course of this period of history, and not only in theoretical terms, but we have also seen real tensions arising. Given that Edinburgh 1910 in its own way stimulated so much renewal in the church, it is natural that we should reflect on its impact and significance.

The future is unpredictable but, from a Christian perspective, remains nonetheless sure. The Christian faith is that the church and all creation are cared for by God. To look forward, then, is to look to God's future, to try to discern where God is pointing. The future that God wills for all creation can be disrupted by human sin, but it can never ultimately be thwarted. For this reason, the Christian can look forward with optimism, with confidence, with trust and with enduring faith. The Christian calling in looking forward is to discern God's will, and to do so requires serious reflection on scripture and on the experience of God's people in the past.

In the course of the many missionary conferences and ecumenical gatherings over the years since 1910, there has been ample reflection on scripture and experience. The spiritual dimension to all the thinking and planning has not been neglected. Time and again in history it has been reflection on scripture that has steered the church in a new direction, or has held the church steady in times of turmoil. The Edinburgh missionary conference of 1910 paid due attention to such spiritual priorities and always, be it in missionary or ecumenical contexts, the experience of being together around scripture, in prayer, in sharing holy communion, in bearing one another's burdens, has brought a wholly new dimension to the thinking and, indeed, has led to unexpected developments and conclusions. We have seen those in this historical survey.

The journey from Edinburgh 1910 to the year 2010 has been a journey that has in many ways exceeded expectations and has brought new insights and approaches that had not been foreseen, turns in the course of things that have taken by surprise. The Spirit renews and changes not only people but also processes. This has been seen time and again over the past century in missionary and ecumenical life: the realisation has dawned on people that there is a different way that is in fact a better way. That is why it was so swiftly understood that the impetus given by Edinburgh 1910 to co-operation among missionary societies should in fact be mirrored in more co-operative and deeper relationships between the churches themselves. The reality of the truth that mission and unity belong together became apparent and it literally drove people forward in the various movements – in the International Missionary Council, in Faith and Order, in Life and Work, in the World Council of Churches, in the Second Vatican Council. It is not merely the acceptance of change, but much more, the embracing of change that is needed for renewal. 'Conversion' itself implies the adopting of a new direction, and actually travelling in that direction. The missionary and ecumenical movements of the twentieth and now early twenty-first centuries have relied on prophetic leadership, and that prophetic leadership has not been wanting. Women and men from one decade to another have seen how both movements needed to be brought forward, and the initiative was seized, the vision communicated and change embraced.

It is salutary to recall that the future as it was seen at Edinburgh 1910 – now our past – was not the future that came. Far from it. The future that was envisaged with such energy, commitment and unquestioned ambition was of one, fully evangelised world, a world in which western civilisation would come to dominate and in which the Christian faith, concomitantly, would sweep across all peoples. Instead, the century that lay ahead saw two world wars and many other conflicts, the rise and decline of communism, and the church facing immense dangers. The twentieth century was a century of war and peace, economic depression and recovery, totalitarianism and the popular response, scientific advance and western religious decline. It was a century in which the vision of Edinburgh 1910 simply could not happen and, for that reason, the conference marked a high point of missionary expectation and planning to which it would not return. Despite this, however, Edinburgh 1910 had its abiding fruits and we will do well to pause briefly and consider the 'minuses' and 'pluses' of Edinburgh 1910, thereby hopefully learning lessons for today and gaining insights for mission and unity priorities.

'Minuses'

It is easy to see things that were wrong when one looks at past events with hindsight; nonetheless, it is far from fruitless to identify where things went wrong, as long as one understands that people at the time did not have the advantage that we have today, the advantage of experience and of assessing shifting perspectives over intervening years. From our survey of the Edinburgh conference itself, it is clear that certain approaches necessarily limited its scope and vision.

Looked at from today's perspective, the outlook of Edinburgh 1910 was founded on the concept of the world as clearly divided between Christian and non-Christian lands. Brian Stanley writes: 'The World Missionary Conference's division of the world into two sharply delineated geographical sectors – Christian and non-Christian – is the aspect of the conference that became outdated more quickly than any other, and which strikes the twenty-first-century observer as most obviously unacceptable. The first insistent question marks to be placed over the conceptual juxtaposition of Christian west and non-Christian east appeared within a few years of the conference, with the outbreak of war in Europe.'[1]

---

1. B. Stanley, *The World Missionary Conference, Edinburgh 1910*, op. cit., p 304

Kosuke Koyama writes yet more abruptly that 'Edinburgh 1910 was a missiological monologue within the Christian West ... The missionary geography of two worlds, Christian and non-Christian, was facile.'[2]

The close association of church with nation, of Christian faith with western culture, placed hope in the wrong place, in the rise and fall of nations and empires. The kingdom of God is not of this world, but transcends this world with its wholly different values and its eternal dimension. The Edinburgh 1910 outlook thus was one that largely depended on the expanding influence of western culture, embracing, as it did, the Christian religion. While at the time this may have seemed a reasonable outlook, in reality it was a fragile and vulnerable hope because what makes Christianity strong is not its association with worldly powers but precisely its independence from such powers, its ability to challenge such powers and its commitment first and foremost, not to a culture, but to the faith itself and to Christ alone.

For the church today it is important to recognise the need to place hope for the future not in the political constructs of this world but in the proclamation of the gospel itself by word and service, looking first to that responsibility. Indeed, in the post-modern western culture of today, there is the temptation to follow in its way, adapting the Christian faith to more relativistic values. Perhaps we might say that one of the lessons of Edinburgh 1910 and the then unanticipated particular nature of the subsequent growth of the church during the twentieth century, is precisely not to ally faith and culture. Faith must relate to surrounding cultures, of course, but it must retain its distinctive character and hold fast to its central convictions. Otherwise, religion simply becomes an aspect of culture, or even becomes subservient to culture, and therefore cannot bring fundamental renewal to culture. Edinburgh 1910 would not have seen Christianity in the west as counter-cultural in any sense, and in mission lands it was less a case of being counter-cultural in the sense of bringing a critique to

---

2. Kosuke Koyama, *Commission One after a Century of Violence: The Search for a Larger Christ*, in eds D. A. Kerr and K. R. Ross, *Edinburgh 2010: Mission Then and Now*, Oxford: Regnum Books, 2009, p 41

existing culture, and more a case of invading one culture with another. The opposite is the church's calling: it is here as Christ's
body to bring light and truth into a world that is searching for
those eternal things, to exercise a faith-based critique of culture
and to help culture forward to its next manifestation in ways that
align with the values of the kingdom.

Christianity, or indeed religion generally, while culturally influenced, is not essentially a cultural expression; it is a spiritual expression that can and does influence culture, or can even largely
establish a culture. However, the church is not a cultural form but
is a wholly other reality. Christianity and culture are therefore two
separate and distinct impulses in human experience, the former
having at the heart of its mission the renewal of the human community and the influencing of human affairs with the truths that it
professes. This illustrates the ever-renewing power of grace and
the nature of the ever-renewing calling of the church as it finds itself in cultures of each and every generation and place.

Edinburgh 1910, with its rather monochrome 'Christendom'
model, simply did not do justice to these deeper truths about the
church and its vocation and mission. Indeed, the composition of
the conference itself was overwhelmingly western and not sufficiently global in scope, with only 17 of the 1,200 delegates coming
from the 'native' churches. However, that said, it is notable that
those few non-western voices that were heard at Edinburgh made
a very significant impact with their challenging perspectives and,
indeed, J. S. Friesen comments: 'The seventeen members from the
younger churches were accorded positions on the programme
quite out of proportion to their number: out of forty-seven public
addresses given at noon and in the evenings, they presented six.'[3]
More of this would have been even better.

Quite apart from the model of church with which Edinburgh
1910 operated, and its overly western composition, the confer-

---

3. J. S. Friesen, *Missionary Responses to Tribal Religions at Edinburgh 1910*,
New York: Peter Lang, 1996, p 25, as in D. A. Kerr and K. R. Ross,
Edinburgh 2010: Mission Then and Now, Oxford: Regnum Books, 2009,
pp 76f

ence also had an understanding of mission that was somewhat restricted; it was too narrowly concerned with method and strategy, despite all the surrounding confidence and enthusiasm. The view of mission straightforwardly in terms of response to the mandate of Christ did not do justice to the truth that the *missio Dei* approach later brought to influence, that mission is primarily not the activity of Christians or of the church even, but rather of God. In its missionary endeavour, the church must constantly be striving to be a faithful participant in that divine mission, fulfilling its dominically entrusted vocation while also searching for, and identifying with, God's own life and activity in the world.

Then again, the essentially strategic approach of the conference was based on the work of very independent missionary societies and there was no real sense of urgency about mission as fundamentally belonging to the churches as institutions; there was a separateness here that did not 'add up' ecclesiologically, however effective missionary societies could be. Moreover, even Edinburgh 1910's strategy was flawed because, as Stanley also points out, the relatively slight attention given to Africa at the conference 'was congruent with the racial assumptions of the day and with the fact that Africa took second place to India and East Asia in the respective priorities of British and American missions for many years to come'.[4] However, while Stanley records that concepts of racial distinctiveness and variation were integral to the language of the Edinburgh reports, he also, and more happily, stresses how Edinburgh 1910, despite its basic western cultural assumption, nonetheless also showed enthusiasm for 'indigenous agency and cultural diversity in the expression of the Christian faith, and [in] its opposition to imperial exploitation of indigenous peoples'.[5]

Of course, the participation of only 200 women in the 1910 conference was, by contemporary standards, limited, although women's participation in many church structures still lacks proper proportion today. Here it is all too easy to apply modern insights in criticism of another age, and it is true that one of the fruits of the

4. Stanley, *The World Missionary Conference, Edinburgh 1910,* op. cit., p 306f
5. Ibid., p 309

conference was in fact the opening up of opportunities for women to study and train for missionary work.

The language and mindset of Edinburgh 1910, as Kenneth Ross has observed, was very much that of 'the church militant', a concept of the Christian faith as battling for the allegiance of the world and the overcoming of other faiths.[6] The report of the conference's commission on 'Carrying the gospel to all the non-Christian World' could indicate as one of its outstanding convictions that 'the time is also at hand when the church should enter the so-called *unoccupied fields of the world*'. [Italics original] It also stated: 'Whatever can be done should be done which will result in still further developing the power of initiative, of aggressive evangelism, and of self-denying missionary outreach on the part of the Christians of Asia and Africa, and in raising up an army of well-qualified native evangelists and leaders.'[7]

This kind of militaristic language was quite undiluted, presenting a model of religions in confrontation, of missionaries as 'soldiers', as in Charles Wesley's eighteenth century hymn, 'Soldiers of Christ, arise, and put your armour on'. Teresa Okure writes in this connection: 'Mission is not about conquest but God's reconciliation and proclamation of the good news of liberation to all nations. No nation is to be conquered by another, even for Christ. This conquering attitude, located in the colonial mentality, justifies the observation of African scholars that the early missionary enterprise served in many respects as a handmaid of colonialism.'[8]

It is precisely the concept of religions as battling each other that not only is an outdated model in today's context in which dialogue and respect are the keynotes but also sidelines such themes as service and, even, charity. It reveals a presumptuous and almost threatening attitude, even though, at heart, it springs from a conviction of the truth of the gospel and a zeal for communicating

6. Kenneth R. Ross, *Edinburgh 2010: Springboard for Mission*, Pasadena, California: William Carey International University Press, 2009, p 31
7. Gairdner, op. cit., pp 81, 84f
8. T. Okure, *The Church in the Mission Field: A Nigerian/African Response*, in ed D. A. Kerr and K. R. Ross, *Edinburgh 2010: Mission Then and Now*, Oxford: Regnum Books, 2009, p 61

its good news. Of course, also, in the light of the sheer suffering and utter destruction wrought by military conflict, any analogy of mission with war is not merely unfortunate but actually wholly misplaced.

While Edinburgh 1910 consciously and deliberately excluded any discussion of theology or matters of doctrine in order to allow its proceedings to focus on strategy, and to that extent succeeded, there was a price. That price was an inability to consider mission in the light precisely of its content and substance. Certainly, to have proceeded along such lines would have made for a wholly different conference, and quite probably also one less comprehensive in its participation, yet a fundamental dimension to the issue was missing.

'Pluses'

In his reflection on Edinburgh 1910/2010, Kenneth Ross, while also acknowledging such negative aspects of the conference as we have highlighted, refers to 'imagination' as one of its features which carry particular resonance today. This is very productive insight, because the church today, in considering its missionary calling, needs imagination in abundance. While Ross writes that the conference was 'over-ambitious' in many respects, and 'carried away by the self-confidence of the western powers at the height of the age of empire' with its slogans ultimately proving 'hollow', nonetheless he also writes: 'Never did the modern missionary movement articulate its ambition more comprehensively than at Edinburgh 1910. It was a moment of imagination when people came together to think seriously about something which had never existed before: what a truly worldwide church would look like and how it would exercise its missionary obligations.'[9]

Imagination is essential if new ways forward are to be found in whatever context; the alternative is the *status quo* and stagnation. Lack of imagination leaves one enslaved to inherited ways, to 'how things always have been done', and to an attitude, ultimately,

---

9. Kenneth R. Ross, *Edinburgh 2010: Springboard for Mission*, Pasadena, California: William Carey International University Press, 2009, pp 33 and 37

of complacency. A complacent church is a denial of joy in the faith, of any real desire to share the good news. Self-satisfaction is always the danger of such a comfortable church, a church that sees no need for change and has no drive to extend the kingdom of God itself. In the end, a lack of faith sets in, denying the church the spirit that itself makes the church a place where people want to be and rendering the church an institution lacking in the life and action which actually draw people into its fellowship.

The 'minuses' that we have considered suggest that the predominating mood of Edinburgh 1910 was one of conformity to the outlook of the times, but Ross is correct to point out how the conference not only did reveal a confidence about the future, and an energy arising from the recognition of the opportunity of the time, but also possessed the imagination to see how things could be, and the commitment to seek to take the steps that were considered necessary to turn that imagination into reality.

The way in which the planners of Edinburgh 1910 took great care to ensure a broad representation of the actual missionary societies, and of church leaders, itself witnessed to a certain inclusive approach to the missionary task. In bringing together people of very disparate theological outlooks, from Baptist to Anglo-Catholic, the organisers had broken a definite mould. That had required imagination and, indeed, courage. The setting out of the agenda of Edinburgh under eight commissions, each covering a vital area of concern, again witnessed to imagination; the comprehensiveness of the approach not only attested to competence on the part of the organisers but also to their determination to bring the fundamental concerns of the missionary movement together, at one time and in one place, so that they could be properly addressed by the delegates present.

There had been imagination in the way the missionary leaders of the day sought to seize the new opportunities that were presenting themselves for the advance of mission, in the context of a world opening up to travel and communication. Here, surely, lie many lessons for the church of today, because the world of the twenty-first century is one in which there are many new opportunities for Christian outreach and communication. Serene Jones, president of New York's Union Theological Seminary, told a recent meeting of the US National Council of Churches' communications commission that contemporary changes involving media and global communications could prove to be as dramatic for the church as the development of the printing press had been in the fifteenth century. She suggested that Johannes Gutenberg's printing press and the consequent ability to mass produce the Bible had changed not only the terms of communications, but also the understanding of what it means to be human. 'New communities are being formed ... The internet is quickly replacing the communities we used to call churches, with the result that communities of faith exist in a world of "overwhelming transitions", leading to fear and exhaustion,' she said.[10] Certainly, the opportunites that were seen by the mission leaders at the beginning of the twentieth century could well be seen in not dissimilar terms, for it was a world of such transitions as had never before been seen as at all possible, not least in terms of industrialisation and, even, militarisation. Into such a world of unprecedented developments came the missionary societies with their ambitions and their confidence.

This brings us to what is perhaps an allied 'plus' of Edinburgh 1910 – its dynamism. The representatives of the missionary societies came together in Edinburgh to confer, not on abstract subjects, but on the practical way forward for the missionary endeavour in a world of immense opportunity. How could those opportunities best be exploited for the purposes of mission? That was a burning question for representatives who were fired with enthusiasm for the cause of Christ and who were prepared to make real sacrifices in fulfilling their missionary calling. This was a very purpose-driven conference and the dynamism is palpable even one hundred years later. Perhaps it was over-ambitious, perhaps it was not entirely realistic, but it was serious and focused and driven. Timothy Yates, while admitting a certain note of 'world conquest' in the chairman John Mott's closing address at Edinburgh 1910, nonetheless also writes that Mott overall in his speech 'struck a note of firm resolve rather than any optimistic triumphalism',

10. *Ecumenical News International* report by Chris Herlinger, 7 October 2009

adding that the conference had been '*par excellence*, a conference on expansion and extension'.[11] It was such a combination of firm resolve and sheer faith itself that gave Edinburgh 1910 a dynamic quality that, in the end, was to bear many and various fruits. There is similar resolve today in many quarters of the Christian church, but in other quarters – particularly in the west – the church is spending much time and energy on internal divisions. In the latter case, a new focus on mission, such as presents itself with the centenary of Edinburgh 1910, provides a necessary expanding of horizons. This new focus on mission throws one back to the essentials of the faith and also encourages the question as to just how much Christians today in the west want to share the faith or, indeed, really have the confidence in the faith that is necessary if one is to go out and seek to share it and propagate it.

The closing years of the twentieth century were observed by Anglicans as a 'Decade of Evangelism' and by Roman Catholics as a 'Decade of Evangelisation'. Despite the difference in terminology, both programmes were intended to be dynamic. Resolution 43 of the 1988 Lambeth Conference of Anglican bishops stated: 'This Conference, recognising that evangelism is the primary task given to the church, asks each province and diocese of the Anglican Communion, in co-operation with other Christians, to make the closing years of this millennium a "Decade of Evangelism" with a renewed and united emphasis on making Christ known to the people of his world.' Pope John Paul II, in his 1990 encyclical, *Redemptoris Missio*, declared: 'God is opening before the church the horizons of a humanity more fully prepared for the sowing of the gospel. I sense that the moment has come to commit all of the church's energies to a new evangelisation and to the mission *ad gentes*. No believer in Christ, no institution of the church can avoid this supreme duty: to proclaim Christ to all peoples.' The Pope also reflected in his encyclical on how, as a result of his wide travels and direct contact 'with peoples who do not know Christ', he had become even more convinced of the urgency of mission.[12]

While it has been difficult to assess the success or otherwise of

---

11. T. Yates, *Christian Mission in the Twentieth Century*, CUP 1994, pp 31f
12. *Redemptoris Missio*, 3 and 1

that Decade, it is becoming clearer that it led on to new experiments in mission, such as 'fresh expressions of church' and 'church planting'. It took some time for the concepts behind evangelism to become clear in people's minds and it is fair to say that while many look back on that Decade with a certain degree of scepticism, a consciousness of mission was created that put down a serious marker at the turn of the millennium. There was a sense of urgency about mission, not least in Pope John Paul's words, and the highly secular way in which western society was developing also served to underline the need for outreach in new and creative ways. Can such a momentum – if that is not too big a word for the Decade – be sustained in the longer term? Perhaps a lesson of Edinburgh 1910 is that if the church wants programmes sustained, it has to plan very well accordingly. Vision and strategy, enthusiasm and planning are all needed to bring hopes and ambitions, by God's grace, to some form of reality.

Compared with the relatively straightforward thinking of Edinburgh 1910 regarding mission itself, it is true, as Wilbert Shenk comments, that the church in the West today is confused about mission.[13] There is an urgent need to clear up any confusion and the centenary of Edinburgh 1910 provides a real opportunity not only, as D. A. Kerr and K. R. Ross suggest, for the ecumenical and evangelical streams in missiological understanding 'to re-engage with the Edinburgh 1910 heritage and with each other',[14] but also for a new clarity about mission to emerge. The Anglican Communion's 'Five Marks of Mission' provide a concise basis,[15] but in such circumstances, one really is driven back to basics. Christ's prayer for the unity of the church is so that the world may

---

13. W. R. Shenk, *Training Missiologists for Western Culture*, in *Changing Frontiers of Mission*, American Society of Missiology Series, No 28, Maryknoll, New York: Orbis Books 1999, pp 129-138

14. Eds D. A. Kerr and K. R. Ross, *Edinburgh 2010: Mission Then and Now*, Oxford: Regnum Books, 2009, p 41

15. To proclaim the Good News of the Kingdom; To teach, baptise and nurture new believers; To respond to human need by loving service; To seek to transform unjust structures of society; To strive to safeguard the integrity of creation and sustain and renew the life of the earth. (*Mission in a Broken World: Report of ACC-8*, p 101)

believe (Jn 17:21), and it is, in fact, a new vision of a believing world – a contemporary variation on the Edinburgh 1910 theme, indeed – that is necessary for a clearer understanding of the church's enduring mission to emerge for this twenty-first century.

Index